'It is the pervasive presence of anger in criminal courts that best epitomises the emotionality of doing justice. In this brilliant study of four legal systems, Stina Bergman Blix and Nina Törnqvist shed light on the vagaries of this primordial emotion in the courtroom: the paradoxes of substance and formality of justice, moral outrage and judicial restraint, functional rationality and irrationality. This quintessential study is a quantum leap in our understanding of the complex nature of emotions and the law.'

Susanne Karstedt, *Professor in Criminology, Griffith University, Australia*

'A fascinating and highly readable account of the role anger plays in four distinct legal systems. The international comparisons are eye opening! A terrific addition to the literature on the role of emotion in the law.'

Susan A. Bandes, *Centennial Professor of Law Emeritus, DePaul University College of Law, USA*

'This book is a fine piece of research that helps us understand what anger does in our world, revealing that even at the heart of the supposedly rational legal profession, anger can be used to solve problems and make good decisions.'

Mary Holmes, *Professor of Emotions and Society, University of Edinburgh, United Kingdom*

Rational Anger

Exploring the rationales behind legal anger, its logic and origins, this book builds on the perspectives of judges and prosecutors in Italy, Sweden, the United States, and Scotland.

When do judges and prosecutors become angry in court, what do they become angry about, and which other emotions open up for anger? Anger brings people to court and is essential in evaluating wrongdoing and attributing blame, but at the same time, anger is seen as a threat to well-reasoned and just decision-making. Drawing on observations, interviews, and shadowing of legal professionals, the text demonstrates how anger is entangled with legal thought and comes into play in legal practices. By comparing the workings and displays of anger found in different legal systems and emotional cultures, the book elucidates assumptions about law, morality, truth, and emotions that we commonly take for granted.

Rational Anger will be of great interest to students and scholars of criminology, criminal justice, sociology, law, social psychology, and organisation studies.

Stina Bergman Blix is Professor of Sociology at Uppsala University. She studies emotions in professional work, rationality, law, theatre, and qualitative methods. She is principal investigator of an international comparative project (JUSTEMOTIONS) funded by the European Research Council investigating the emotive-cognitive process of judicial decision-making. Her work has been published in journals such as *Symbolic Interaction*, *Emotion Review*, and *Qualitative Research* and she co-authored *Professional Emotions in Court: A Sociological Perspective* (Routledge, 2018).

Nina Törnqvist has a PhD in Criminology from Stockholm University and is a researcher at the Department of Sociology at Uppsala University. Her main research interests include legal professionals, emotions, victimology, narratives, and qualitative methods. After working in the JUSTEMOTIONS project, she is currently engaged in research projects on *The emotional dynamic of police and crime victim interactions in IPV investigations* and on *Justice and accountability for business involvement in international crimes.*

Routledge Frontiers of Criminal Justice

Holistic Responses to Reduce Reoffending
Ian Mahoney and Rahmanara Chowdhury

Policing Rape
The Way Forward
Katrin Hohl and Elizabeth A. Stanko

Human Rights in Probation
Theory, Practice and Balance
Kyros Hadjisergis

Corporate Criminal Liability and Sanctions
Current Trends and Policy Changes
Edited by Michala Meiselles, Nicholas Ryder and Arianna Visconti

Crime Prevention by Exclusion
Ethical Considerations
Edited by Sebastian Jon Holmen, Thomas Søbirk Petersen & Jesper Ryberg

Occupational Stress Injuries
Operational and Organizational Stressors Among Public Safety Personnel
Edited by Rosemary Ricciardelli, Joy C. MacDermid and Lorna Ferguson

Mass Data Surveillance and Predictive Policing
Contested Foundations and Human Rights Impact
Plixavra Vogiatzoglou

Rational Anger
An International Comparison of Legal Systems
Stina Bergman Blix and Nina Törnqvist

For more information about this series, please visit: www.routledge.com/Routledge-Frontiers-of-Criminal-Justice/book-series/RFCJ

Rational Anger

An International Comparison of Legal Systems

Stina Bergman Blix and Nina Törnqvist

Routledge
Taylor & Francis Group
LONDON AND NEW YORK

First published 2025
by Routledge
4 Park Square, Milton Park, Abingdon, Oxon OX14 4RN

and by Routledge
605 Third Avenue, New York, NY 10158

Routledge is an imprint of the Taylor & Francis Group, an informa business

British Library Cataloguing-in-Publication Data
A catalogue record for this book is available from the British Library

Library of Congress Cataloging-in-Publication Data
Names: Blix, Stina Bergman, author. | Törnqvist, Nina, author.
Title: Rational anger : an international comparison of legal systems / Stina Bergman Blix and Nina Törnqvist.
Description: First. | Abingdon, Oxon [UK] ; New York, NY : Routledge, 2025. | Series: Routledge frontiers of criminal justice | Includes bibliographical references and index.
Identifiers: LCCN 2024051896 (print) | LCCN 2024051897 (ebook) | ISBN 9781032361765 (hardback) | ISBN 9781032361772 (paperback) | ISBN 9781003330592 (ebook)
Subjects: LCSH: Practice of law--Italy--Psychological aspects. | Practice of law--Sweden--Psychological aspects. | Practice of law--United States--Psychological aspects. | Practice of law--Scotland--Psychological aspects. | Judges--Psychology. | Public prosecutors--Psychology. | Comparative law. | Anger.
Classification: LCC K346 .B55 2025 (print) | LCC K346 (ebook) | DDC 340/.19--dc23/eng/20241104
LC record available at https://lccn.loc.gov/2024051896
LC ebook record available at https://lccn.loc.gov/2024051897

ISBN: 978-1-032-36176-5 (hbk)
ISBN: 978-1-032-36177-2 (pbk)
ISBN: 978-1-003-33059-2 (ebk)

DOI: 10.4324/9781003330592

Typeset in Sabon
by KnowledgeWorks Global Ltd.

Contents

Acknowledgements

First of all, we wish to thank all the judges and prosecutors in this study who so generously have shared their time, feelings, and thoughts with us, inviting us into the secret garden of legal anger. Without you, there would have been no book.

As this book is part of a larger research project, JUSTEMOTIONS, we are immensely grateful to all people involved in this collaboration. Above all, Alessandra Minissale and Cecilia Nordquist who with such dedication have collected and coded the data from Italy, respectively, the United States, and Scotland but also Kemberlee Bonnet for conducting interviews in the United States and Hanna Nir for coding and organising our data. Thanks also to Terry Maroney and Francesco Contini for prosperous support and practical advice. We would also like to express gratitude to the European Research Council for giving us the opportunity to conduct this research and work on this book.

Cultivating the ideas in the book, we owe Klara Hermansson, Karl Malmqvist, and Åsa Wettergren who so kindly read individual chapters and provided thoughtful and enthusiastic comments at various stages of its development. Last but not least, we thank Anna Lund and Isabel Schoultz who took the time and trouble to read the near-final draft and gave us useful suggestions and encouragement. Finally yet importantly, we want to thank David Shannon for his careful review of the language in the book.

1 Introduction

We all know anger and the mess that anger can make – anger tends to come in inconvenient times, interrupting whatever we are doing, and craving our full attention. Anger can be ruthlessly uncompromising and tactless. At the same time, anger can be useful, even precious. When things go wrong, anger can unleash energy, open our eyes, and help us overcome hurdles. While anger is a demanding companion, it can sometimes be necessary for pursuing rational goals.

Anger has attracted a lot of interest in the social sciences and humanities over recent decades (Holmes, 2004; Nussbaum, 2016; Mishra, 2018; Rosenwein, 2020). In the political sphere, anger is often depicted, somewhat pointedly, as either destructive or productive. Modernity, with its global quest for constant growth and control has been labelled an "international economy of disaffection" (Mishra, 2018: 343) that produces destructive *aggression* (Rosa, 2020), with unfulfilled hopes for equality generating violent feelings of *ressentiment*. In social movements research, on the other hand, anger is often depicted as an invigorating emotion that generates agency among oppressed groups (Lorde, 1997; Srinivasan, 2018; Cherry, 2021). *Rage* in the face of inequality finds inspiration in ideas of *righteous anger* in its intentions to level out discriminatory practices and serve the collective good.

Our book explores anger that is both dependent on and decoupled from the political sphere, namely legal anger, or more precisely the way legal professionals use anger in their work. But we do not proceed from a view that anger is either good or bad. This might seem contradictory since the title of the book promises to explore 'rational' anger, a normative claim if ever there was one. Rational can mean many things, but optimal problem-solving lies at the heart of the concept (Brunsson and Brunsson, 2017). In the legal sphere, rational further implies that problem-solving, or the process leading up to a decision, should follow a predefined route (Weber, 1978). Every time a legal matter is investigated and tried in court, the way the legal professionals gather information, solve problems along the way, and evaluate the facts, should be the same for an (optimal) decision to emerge (Bourdieu, 1986; Bergman Blix, 2022). Our take is that rational anger sets out to ensure this predefined or systematic process by the people who are responsible, that is

DOI: 10.4324/9781003330592-1

the legal professionals. The focus on legal professionals is important, since they hold powerful and high-status positions. In combination, the systematic process of solving problems and making decisions, together with the powerful position occupied by legal professionals, make legal anger the prototype of rational anger. Exploring anger in this most rational of conditions may provide theoretical clues into the social construction of anger in more general terms, and it allows us to dissect how anger unfolds within formal processes, where it often goes unnoticed, and importantly, becomes disassociated from its emotional basis. The main contribution of this book lies in elucidating anger as a core junction of diverse legal practices, pushing ideas of fairness, morality, and professionalism to their point. In concrete terms, this means that we do not analyse all the various types of anger felt and displayed by legal professionals. Instead, we narrow our focus to anger that is linked to their systematic efforts to solve legal problems and make decisions in legal practice.

Returning to the political sphere described above, we live in many ways in a world of anger (Mishra, 2018; Rosa, 2020; Rosenwein, 2020). In the legislative sphere, this propensity for anger may have manifested itself in the punitive turn witnessed over recent decades (Garland, 1993), signalling a growing call to exact public retribution on the perpetrators of crime (Karstedt, 2002; Nussbaum, 2016). But how about the judicial sphere? Is societal anger mirrored in our courts? Previous research from the United States and Israel has argued that anger is the most common and least stigmatised emotion among judges and prosecutors (Maroney, 2012; Leiterdorf-Shkedy and Gal, 2019). But anger is also the most problematised emotion in this hyper-rational setting (Maroney, 2012; Bergman Blix and Wettergren, 2018; Roach Anleu and Mack, 2021). This has to do with the fact that legal decision-making should not only follow a systematic process, the process itself should also observe legal principles such as objectivity and impartiality, which are traditionally associated with an absence of emotion (Weber, 1998), with "dispassion" (Maroney, 2011). Furthermore, being professional implies asserting a certain "disinterestedness" (Parsons, 1939: 458), and in a profession that takes pride in rational reasoning, a 'heated' emotion like anger needs to be shunned. This ideal of dispassion is not only deeply embedded in the norms of court interactions (Bergman Blix and Wettergren, 2019), it is also inscribed into judicial codes and professional policies. As an example, a prominent international document on judicial ethics by the United Nations, the Bangalore Principles of Judicial Conduct (UNODC, 2006), maintains that judges should be "patient, dignified and courteous" in relation to all the people they deal with in their official capacity. Another example can be found in the judicial oath given by Swedish judges that state that they will "never manipulate the law or further injustice for kinship, relation by marriage, friendship, envy, ill-will, or fear" (CJP, 1942: Chapter 4, 11 §). Anger, in the form of rudeness or "ill-will", serves as a common ground for complaints about legal conduct (Roach Anleu and Mack, 2021: 65). In other words, while anger may be a part of the art of the legal process, it creates doubt, and may even disrupt core ideals of criminal justice.

It is also important to note that legal anger may be conceived as more or less problematic in different countries. The way the legal system is set up, the foundational rules and regulations that steer the decision-making process, is likely to influence the way anger plays out (as will be described in the section on *Comparing legal traditions* below), and a nation's emotional culture influences the way anger is expressed within the ideal of dispassion (Wettergren and Bergman Blix, 2021). In this book, we compare legal anger in four different countries and legal systems, Sweden, Italy, the United States, and Scotland, to account for the ways in which legal traditions and the general emotional expressiveness of a specific culture affect the unfolding of anger in court.

Anger in context

To understand anger's role in legal practice, we need to place it within its situational and cultural context. Aristotle was early to observe that anger needs to be strictly controlled in order to be used "at the right times, with reference to the right objects, towards the right people, with the right aim, and in the right way" (in Rosenwein, 2020: 82). For legal anger to be what the legal scholar Terry Maroney has described as *righteous*, the judge needs to abide by detailed feeling rules (Hochschild, 1983) regarding when, how, and for what purposes anger should be used. However, in its original Christian version, righteous anger was a divine right, eventually delegated to kings, *ira regis*, and the nobility as a result of their assumed proximity to God (Rosenwein, 1998). This connects righteous anger to powerful positions, symbolised in the legal sphere by the state's monopoly of violence. Righteous legal anger relies on the idea that law functions as a buffer against ordinary people acting out retaliatory anger in the form of vigilantism (Belleau et al., 2008).[1] Judges, with their executive power, serve as "society's anger surrogates" (Maroney, 2012: 1209). But the divine link also points to righteous anger, or *wrath*, as having the aim of "restraining sin" (Rosenwein, 2020: 104). If anger constitutes an assessment that a relationship has gone wrong (Fischer and Roseman, 2007), anger can be justified by its moral aim to restore community. In this way, the righteously angry judge acknowledges the sinner's "moral agency" (Maroney, 2012: 1258) and ability to change, and communicates care by trying to reintegrate "sinners" into society (Braithwaite, 1989). If we follow this logic in the other direction, judges who do not feel anger in the face of wrongdoing would be signalling

1 This is also an important point in the argument for the usefulness of rage as a means of changing discriminatory social structures. If subordinate groups violate the feeling rules that only allow anger by superior groups, the anger itself constitutes a challenge to the current social order (Cherry, 2021).

that they lack a sense of community with the people they are set up to judge, feeling indifferent instead of angry. In Chapter 2, *Nagging narratives*, we show that legal professionals do indeed communicate care in legal proceedings, but that their care is mainly directed at ensuring that the stories told in court enables them to make correct decisions. Legal anger sets out to encourage narratives that are fit for legal evaluations and assessments, while at the same time allowing for credible stories that tend to remain messy, which is demonstrated by efforts to balance between expressing and withholding anger.

The key problem with the notion of rational anger is its association with losing control. The ancient philosopher Seneca was early to argue that anger, or *ira* "bent [reason] out of shape" (Rosenwein, 2020: 26), and anger remains figuratively associated with insanity, being viewed as making us boil or smoulder – a natural force about to be unleashed (Kövecses, 2000). Disruptive anger is a fiery, explosive emotion associated with impulsiveness, irrational behaviour, and aggression. In this way, anger constitutes the epitome of emotions as being opposite to reason – as basic, primitive affect. This is a reputation that makes anger a suspicious phenomenon in the high-status, civilised, and composed setting of the courtroom. In Chapter 3 on *Timely temper*, we will problematise this idea of anger as an explosive and short-tempered emotion, exploring how anger in court is shaped to fit with legal norms and tasks in its release, duration, and intensity. Anger is systematically postponed to befit problem-solving, may be swift or long lasting depending on the task at hand, and unfolds alongside other emotions, such as surprise and confidence. For this, we need to move beyond a simplistic characterisation of anger both in its conceptual definition and by incorporating a range of angry feelings that resemble each other, such as rage, indignation, frustration, and irritation, as they convey meanings of dislike and disapproval for actions or behaviours in "a complex bundle" (Maroney, 2012: 1223).

Defining anger

We all know anger, and we all know that anger can make us want to do different things depending on when and where we feel it. Might a closer look at how anger is defined in more general terms tell us something about legal anger?

At its core, anger involves an assessment of a behaviour as harmful or wrong, together with disapproval of the action that has caused harm (Averill, 1983; Lerner and Tiedens, 2006; Nussbaum, 2016). This means that anger builds on a perception of injustice (Miceli and Castelfranchi, 2019; Sorial, 2019). Depicted in this way, anger involves *appraisals of wrongdoing and harm*, that is identifying what has happened, and whether what has happened constitutes an unwarranted act, and *attributions of blame*, that is identifying who was responsible. These features lie at the very core of the legal process and are precisely what we expect judges and prosecutors to do. In light of this, it is not surprising that anger has been claimed to be "the quintessentially judicial emotion" (Maroney, 2012: 1208–1209).

To tease apart this claim, we need to add another component to the anger process. Anger includes both backward- and forward-looking evaluation, looking back at the harm done and looking forward to correct it (Nussbaum, 2016). These evaluations come together to form a "readiness to act", or in other words, action tendencies (Frijda, 1986). Anger motivates an urge to change a situation, and to be able to take control. This does not mean that we necessarily act on this urge, but the links between anger, confidence, and certainty can fuel agency (Lerner and Tiedens, 2006). Anger tends to move us towards rather than away from something. Although, the aim of this agency-towards is debated. One view, originating from the antique thinkers Aristotle and Seneca, argues that anger incorporates attack tendencies with retributive aims in the form of "being prepared to retaliate" (Deonna and Teroni, 2015: 303), or "payback" (Nussbaum, 2016: 46). This constitutional role of *retribution* in anger has been challenged by researchers who stress the "energy [of anger as] serving progress and recognition" (Lorde, 1997), arguing that the constitutional aim of anger is *recognition* of harm (Silva, 2024). In this view, we do not primarily want to hurt the person who has hurt us, but for anger to subside, we need them to recognise that they have hurt us. But if legislative aims encourage retribution, does this imply that legal professionals embrace retributive action tendencies in their work? The short answer on the basis of our data is no, payback anger is rare, but the longer answer is, it depends. In Chapter 4 on *Respectable rage*, we show how conceptualisations of the aims and understanding of legal anger vary between different legal systems and emotional regimes. Distinguishing between moral outrage, the condemnation of offences, and legal pathos, the promotion of a just process, we find differences in the direction of moral anger and in whether it instigates action tendencies towards retribution, recognition, or resignation.

Finally, and to add to our original intention of studying rational anger without taking a normative stance, and although it may perhaps be stating the obvious, we need to make the point that anger is an inherent part of both human interaction in general and professional legal interaction. Despite the fact that anger may come across as an alien and inappropriate emotion in the legal setting, it nonetheless saturates this social space in multifaceted and ubiquitous ways. Being 'against anger' on principle would simply amount to avoiding understanding how it works. Instead of starting out with an unrealistic ideal of rational practice as being devoid of anger, we want to explore how anger is made rational in the everyday solving of legal problems in our courts. In our final *Discussion* chapter, we will address anger's strengths and weaknesses in relation to the management of legal problems, and highlight the importance of perspective in understanding the role of legal anger and the directions it takes.

Law and anger – insights from previous research

At the heart of Sidney Lumet's classical and much praised film from 1957, *12 Angry Men*, lies a struggle between the way the emotion of anger may be conducive or harmful to the process of achieving justice. Depicting a deliberation involving twelve (all) white, (all) male jurors who are trying to agree on a verdict in a murder case, the movie engages in questions about the significance of doubt, the relevance of moral evaluations, and the importance of disagreement in the collective pursuit of legal justice. During this process, all of the jurors flare up in passionate anger to defend their opinions about how the case should be decided. In one scene, Juror Number 7, an impatient salesman, suddenly changes his mind from voting guilty to not guilty, with no other motive than that he simply wants to reach a decision quickly, so that he can make it to a baseball game. In response, Juror Number 11, a well-mannered watchmaker, bursts out in a passionate speech: "YOU HAVE SAT HERE AND VOTED GUILTY WITH EVERYONE ELSE BECAUSE THERE ARE SOME BASEBALL TICKETS BURNING A HOLE IN YOUR POCKET. NOW YOU HAVE CHANGED YOUR VOTE BECAUSE YOU'RE SICK OF ALL THE TALKING HERE?" At the end of this rant, he walks in a demonstratively hostile way towards Juror Number 7: "WHO TELLS YOU THAT YOU HAVE THE RIGHT TO PLAY LIKE THIS WITH A MAN'S LIFE?"

Breaking with the dominant imperative for legal dispassion, this scene illustrates the importance of anger in protecting central legal values. Juror Number 11's boiling anger is aligned with ideals of legal pathos, and with respect for the gravity of a trial and what is at stake for the parties involved. This call for strong legal emotions also dominates the pioneering work presented in Susan Bandes' edited collection *The Passions of the Law* (1999). Since then, the research on law and emotion has rapidly matured into a full-bodied and rich scholarship, which refutes the long-standing idea of emotions as only being undesirable and dysfunctional in relation to the legal system (Maroney, 2011; Bandes and Blumenthal, 2012; Bergman Blix and Wettergren, 2024). One tenet of contemporary socio-legal studies in this field is that emotions are ubiquitous in the legal sphere, not only as an essential aspect of the experiences of people who encounter the criminal justice system as defendants, plaintiffs, or witnesses but as an equally indispensable part of the everyday reality of legal professionals (Maroney and Gross, 2014; Bandes et al., 2021). In line with Juror Number 11's ardent outburst in *12 Angry Men*, several law and emotion scholars have noted that a deep respect for the law (Tiscione, 2019), conceptualised as legal pathos (Minissale, 2023), provides an essential motivation for legal professionals, since faith and trust in the legal system are what makes their work meaningful and worthwhile. Without these emotions, legal practice would be lacking in relation to both motivation and goals.

While the field of law and emotion covers a wide range of emotions, in this brief overview we will zoom in on existing socio-legal research that has dealt with anger in the legal sphere. In order to provide a broader understanding of the empirical findings presented in the following chapters, we delve into three strands of research: the dynamics of anger in courtroom interactions, emotion management and different forms of 'anger work' among legal professionals, and lastly, the role of anger in legal decision-making.

Anger in court

As Maroney (2012) has argued, the legal working environment is full of situations that commonly elicit anger related to the exercise of power and hostile interactions. Within the field of law and emotion, the commonality of occurrences of anger becomes particularly evident in the many studies that have focused on courtroom interaction (see for example Scarduzio, 2011; Bergman Blix and Wettergren, 2018; Flower, 2020; Roach Anleu and Mack, 2021) but anger has rarely been scrutinised as the sole focus of the research (for an exception, see Maroney, 2012). As mentioned above, anger relates to some form of perceived hurt, and one might ask oneself what kind of hurt legal anger pertains to. Previous research shows that judges and other legal professionals become angry in instances of "incompetence, disrespect, unwarranted harm inflicted on others, and lies" (Maroney, 2012: 1213). Common triggers of anger include comments or objections that are interpreted as nonsensical drivel and foolishness (Roach Anleu and Mack, 2021: 134–135). Another finding that is echoed in several studies is that actions that are perceived to be detrimental to the legal process elicit anger among legal professionals (Maroney, 2012; Bergman Blix and Wettergren, 2018). Mirroring these findings, various studies also show that anger is used by judges and prosecutors to restore and maintain order in courtroom interactions (Scarduzio, 2011; Roach Anleu and Mack, 2013; Nordquist and Bergman Blix, 2022). Somewhat paradoxically, judicial anger can be used to uphold the civility of the courtroom and protect the safety, dignity, and autonomy of both legal professionals and lay people (Maroney, 2012; Roach Anleu and Mack, 2017).

Understanding emotions as relational (Burkitt, 2014; Cottingham, 2022), different relations in the courtroom are prone to different anger dynamics. While people with more power and status are in general allowed to feel and act out on their anger to a greater extent than people in weaker social positions (Kemper, 1978), the power dynamics that reside in the courtroom are multifaceted and pursue a specific logic (Scarduzio, 2011). Maroney (2012) argues that legal anger is more accepted towards other legal professionals than towards lay people such as defendants, complainants, and witnesses. This can partly be explained by findings showing that legal professionals empathise with lay people's situation in court, understanding that they may experience the courtroom as stressful, which tends to elicit patience rather than anger (Roach Anleu and Mack, 2021: 132). In addition, other studies have noted that prosecutorial anger towards defendants is more accepted than anger directed at complainants (Leiterdorf-Shkedy and Gal, 2019: 12) and that criminal cases that call for compassion for victims (Bandes, 1996) or involve gruesome evidence (Bright and Goodman-Delahunty, 2006) evoke judicial anger towards defendants. Taken together, these studies suggest that expectations of familiarity with the courtroom interaction order (differentiating between professionals and lay people), and social status linked to the criminal event (relating to more general attributions of blame and sympathy in society, cf. Clark, 1997; Kusenbach and Loseke, 2013), both influence the appropriateness of legal anger. Notably, legal professionals need to align their anger with the right ends for it to be "righteous" (Maroney, 2012). While anger may be appropriate for judges as a means of claiming authority (Scarduzio, 2011) and ensuring the prompt compliance of the involved parties (Maroney, 2012; Roach Anleu and Mack, 2017), anger that is expressed to assert dominance and superiority is seen as a breach of professional conduct (Maroney, 2012; see also: Törnqvist, 2017; Bergman Blix and Wettergren, 2018).

Importantly, some anger displays are viewed as an inherent part of legal roles, with defence lawyers, for example, being expected to demonstrate an agile fierceness during a court hearing that involves anger, hostility, and intimidation, thus performing the role of "Rambo litigators" (Pierce, 1995), or in the Swedish context, an emotionally subdued "Rambo Bambi" version (Flower, 2020). In parallel, the main aim of the prosecutor during court proceedings is to prove that the defendant is guilty beyond reasonable doubt, which in many cases involves aggressive and face-threatening acts (Törnqvist, 2017), and judges quite commonly need to deliver "bad news" to defendants and complainants (Roach Anleu and Mack, 2021: 154). In fact, the court proceeding itself might be perceived as a "social degradation ceremony" (Garfinkel, 1956), and both defendants and complainants may experience the trial in terms of social humiliation and loss of agency (Konradi, 1999; Dahlberg, 2009; Bitsch, 2019).

Managing anger

Another pertinent and related strand of research concentrates on the emotion work that legal professionals perform in order to feel and express anger at the right time and in the right way. Studies demonstrate that legal professionals are expected to put their emotions aside, placing their anger in the margins (Bandes, 2021) and remaining cool and displaying a stone face during court proceedings (Bergman Blix and Wettergren, 2019). 'Staying calm', patience, and compassion are emotions that judges use to consciously work on their angry emotions (Roach Anleu and Mack, 2019; 2021). These emotions are not only a way to control and reduce one's own anger, they can also be beneficial in de-escalating a heated situation (Roach Anleu and Mack, 2019: 841). Given tact and timing, humour may serve a similar function, working both as a relief and safety valve, as well as an emotion management technique to take the edge off a turbulent situation (Roach Anleu and Mack, 2021). Legal professionals may also actively remind themselves of core legal values, such as impartiality and appearing impersonal, in order to shift focus and curtail their anger (Maroney, 2012; Roach Anleu and Mack, 2017: 126). Australian and Swedish research has shown that legal professionals who deal with emotionally challenging cases may work on their emotions, including anger and despair, in a safe space, such as their offices, before the trial starts (Törnqvist, 2017; Bergman Blix and Wettergren, 2018; Roach Anleu and Mack, 2021).

Needless to say, the strict emotion (display) rules of the courtroom, also cause legal actors to fail. In a study on municipal court judges in the United States, Jennifer Scarduzio (2011) shows that judges deviate from the emotional expectations of neutrality and fairness in several ways when interacting with defendants. She concludes that both implicit (eye rolling, lack of eye contact, and specific hand gestures) and explicit forms of emotional deviance (displays of humour and anger that are close to rudeness) are common among the anger displays of judges. Resonating with these findings, Maroney's (2012) study on angry judges in the United States indicates the presence of a vivid and expressive emotion regime that allows both 'bench-slapping' and direct, verbal confrontations (Maroney, 2012). In comparison to the overt emotional displays of anger and frustration found in the US legal context, research on Swedish judges and prosecutors shows that emotions in the Swedish courtroom tend to be downplayed or quietened, and take the form of delicate facial and bodily expressions such as raised eyebrows and glances (Bergman Blix and Wettergren, 2016; Flower, 2018). For example, angry judges may demonstrate their anger by putting down their pen, an emotional cue that only 'insiders' would perceive as anger (Bergman Blix and Wettergren, 2016). Another subtle form of anger described in previous research from Australia involves the use of diminutive forms of address, such as 'Miss', which may convey a reprimand or paternalistic condemnation (Roach Anleu and Mack, 2021: 93), but also the use of sarcasm and belittling remarks when a defendant is perceived as disrespectful (Roach Anleu and Mack, 2017). To sum up, previous law and emotion research on the anger of legal professionals in the courtroom shows that this anger is immensely regulated by a complex nexus of emotion rules, and that it thus demands skilled emotion work, but that legal professionals also break with these emotion rules on a more or less regular basis.

Angry deliberations

Turning to the final element of our exposition of previous research, the role of anger in legal decision-making, we will once again revisit the film, *12 Angry Men*. Throughout the movie, the protagonist, Juror Number 8, an elegant architect played by Henry Fonda, pushes the other jurors to go over the evidence together thoroughly, piece by piece. By elucidating ambiguities in the court testimonies, biased assumptions, and professional negligence, Fonda's character demonstrates the other jurors' willingness to distort reality in order to avoid doubt and uncertainty. Fonda's determination to get things right by doing right creates frustration among the other jurors, as when Juror Number 7 confronts Juror 8, "Listen, there are still eleven of us who think he's guilty. You're alone. What do you think you're gonna accomplish? If you want to be stubborn and hang this jury, he'll be tried again and found guilty, sure as he's born". The resistance faced by Juror Number 8 illuminates the challenging task of being the dissenting party in the deliberation room, particularly in an open-and-shut case. In an interview with one of the judges in our study, Ruben (55+, Sweden), he started talking about the importance of everyone who decides a criminal legal case being their own Henry Fonda, reminding themselves to "just wait a moment". Continuing his reasoning, Judge Ruben said: "We all have preconceived notions and ideas about the world ...", but in the deliberation room, everyone should "try to help each other to bring out the best in ourselves and decide ... decide according to the judge's honour", welcoming disagreement and discussion in order to move beyond "the overall impression and gut feelings" in a case.

Judge Ruben's moral take-away from the movie chimes well with a salient strand of research regarding the role of legal anger in criminal legal processes, which focuses on the perils of anger in legal decision-making (Bright and Goodman-Delahunty, 2006; Georges et al., 2013; Feigenson, 2016). Summarising the main findings in this field, Maroney (2012) concludes that anger promotes shallow information processes, comes with a tendency to rely on stereotypes, and may lead to premature or overly punitive decisions. In a legal setting, anger is associated with stronger attributions of intentionality and blame, leaving alternative explanations and mitigating circumstances unaccounted for (Belleau et al., 2008; Simon, 2019). Other studies show that anger seems to reduce evidentiary thresholds (Quigley and Tedeschi, 1996; Goldberg et al., 1999; Keltner et al., 2003) and to generate (over) confidence in decisions (Tiedens and Linton, 2001; Roach Anleu and Mack, 2021).

In one of the most powerful scenes of *12 Angry Men*, Juror Number 10, a racist, short-tempered car mechanic, goes off into a fiery rhetoric, ranting about the accused's lack of credibility on the basis of racial stereotypes. "You're not going to tell me that we're supposed to believe this kid knowing what he is? Listen, I've lived among them all my life. You can't believe a word they say; you know that. I mean they are born liars." As Juror Number 10's prejudiced outburst culminates, everyone else in the jury turns their back on him. They don't express disagreement, they don't even exert themselves to say anything, but their silence speaks volumes. Juror Number 10's inadequate anger does not resonate, and he gradually loses his emotional energy and stumbles out to the periphery of the gathering, sinking down at a small table. The other jurors retake their seats, ready to move forward. The unjust and irrational anger has lost.

In real life, unsound and detrimental anger is not always conquered by more virtuous equivalents, and importantly the distinction between them is not always clear. Our aim in this book is to offer a foundation for a more informed and invigorating discussion about the role of legal anger based on empirical analyses of anger as it evolves in real-world legal decision-making.

Comparing legal traditions

Before we move into the courtroom, we need to address our selection of countries and the legal systems that they represent. In order to illuminate the role of anger in court, we have selected countries that represent different legal traditions with varying degrees of emotional expressiveness. Sweden and Italy represent civil law systems, which are based on systematised, logically connected formal laws, whereas the United States and Scotland represent common law systems, which are based on case law, that is, previous decisions made by judges, so called precedents. Today, these differences are not clear cut, with both civil and common law systems having integrated procedures and principles from one another, but their respective historical roots influence how law is organised, and thus also the outlook of legal professionals and their room for manoeuvre within the system in which they work.

In civil law systems, the emphasis on formal law is meant to lead to a single, coherent way of understanding the law, which legal professionals then apply. Judges should think about the law in standardised terms, applying law to the facts in concrete cases by comparing legal prerequisites with the real event, as presented in the form of factual evidence by the prosecutor (Weber, 1978; Bladini, 2013). In the civil law countries examined here, judging is a career profession. In Italy, but not in Sweden, judges and prosecutors follow the same educational path. In contrast, common law judges are appointed from the ranks of experienced lawyers. Common law practice is expected to develop continuously and to be interpreted in its current social context (Dworkin, 1986: 313–354). Legal professionals should play an active role, not only applying but also making law through precedents. In the United States, the making of law is further emphasised in legal professionals' everyday work, since the heads of prosecution offices, and in several states also judges, are politically elected. For the purpose of studying anger, these foundational differences between common and civil law systems are important, since in civil law systems, the educational paths of judges and prosecutors and the emphasis on applying the law create a distinct gap between law and moral evaluations, whereas the professional mobility found in common law systems, and the focus on interpreting and developing the law, links legal practice to current moral standards. Could this mean that legal professionals in the United States and Scotland are more prone to moral outrage than their Italian and Swedish counterparts?

Morality and truth

The role of moral evaluations in legal proceedings is further complicated by the different approaches to truth and truth-seeking practices in the respective legal systems. In criminal law, the differences between civil and common law are manifested in their use of inquisitorial and adversarial procedures, respectively. Inquisitorial procedure relies on the ideal that an impartial representative of the state investigates (makes a formal *inquisition* into) the criminal case and seeks to reveal substantive truth (Spencer, 2016), while the adversarial procedure instead builds on a competitive foundation, in which two opposing parties are believed to pave the way for revealing the truest version of events (Ambos, 2003; May, 2005). Judges in inquisitorial systems have a duty to actively seek the truth, whereas adversarial judges should not engage in the production of evidence, but merely decide on whether or not the prosecution has proved its case. In this way, legal professionals working with adversarial procedures do not deal with what actually happened (the truth) in the case, only with whether the evidence holds, which ought to serve to counter feelings of moral outrage. In this way, the institutional arrangements of civil law systems may be said to hold back the moral anger of legal professionals through the system's slow evolution and stress on applying the law, while promoting moral outrage through their emphasis on active truth seeking. In contrast, common law systems may be said to promote legal professionals' moral outrage through the way they stress the active development of law and its contextualisation in the present, while holding back moral anger through their emphasis on proof rather than truth.

Having said this, inquisitorial and adversarial practices are not mutually exclusive categories and the countries represented in our data have integrated elements from both. First, all four of the countries in our data share fundamental legal principles and practices, such as the presumption of innocence, the right to counsel, the right to confrontation, and standards of proof, and their court proceedings are all governed by the principles of immediacy and orality. Italy and Sweden have their origins in inquisitorial systems but have integrated several adversarial principles.[2] For example, judges are regarded as passive arbiters in all four countries, but in Italy, judges are allowed to ask for more evidence and to interrogate the accused and the witnesses when they deem this necessary. In Sweden, judges are allowed to ask questions to clarify the case but should avoid questions that may lead to a conviction of the defendant. In both Italy and Sweden, judges follow the principle of the free evaluation of evidence, and Italian and Swedish courts have less strict rules than the United States and Scotland with regard to the submission of evidence. In all four countries, prosecutors

2 In Sweden, a shift towards more adversarial influences occurred via a legal reform in 1948. The Italian criminal justice system went through a larger reform in 1988, adopting several adversarial elements, such as preliminary hearings, cross-examination, and plea bargains.

have a duty to be objective. In Italy and Sweden this includes being responsible for conducting comprehensive investigatory measures and presenting evidence that favours, or even exonerates, the suspect at trial. In the United States and Scotland prosecutors have a clearer adversarial role also during preliminary investigations, potentially balanced by the defence side making their own investigations.

Deliberations

Another important difference between the countries we have selected is that the foundation of civil law in systematised formal law implies that the understanding of the law is reserved for legal professionals, and juries are therefore not used to the extent found in common law systems. When lay judges are involved, they deliberate together with professional judges. In Sweden, one professional judge deliberates together with three lay judges in first instance courts, while three professional judges deliberate together with two lay judges in the appellate court. In Italy, judges in first instance courts make decisions in the context of preliminary investigations, preliminary hearings, and in regular trials. Depending on the type of crime involved, cases are decided by one professional judge or a panel of three judges. In the appellate court, decisions are made by a panel comprising three professional judges and six lay judges. In the United States and Scotland, the majority of cases do not go to trial but are decided via plea bargains, where the accused admits to guilt and a sanction is negotiated between the prosecution and the defence and signed off on by a judge. In the United States, trials can be decided by an individual judge in a bench trial, but most trials are decided by a jury comprising 12 members of the public. In the appellate court, decisions are ordinarily made by a panel of three judges. In Scotland, cases are tried either by a single judge or a 15-member jury. Appeals are heard by panels of two or three judges. In both the Swedish and Italian legal systems, appeals can be made for both factual and legal reasons, while in the United States and Scotland, appeals can ordinarily only be made for legal reasons.

In Italy and Sweden, professional judges, sometimes together with lay judges, make decisions on both guilt and the sanction in the same trial. In the United States and Scotland decisions on guilt are in most cases decided by a jury (if the case goes to trial), with the sentence being determined in a separate process, most often by a professional judge. In Italy, the United States, and Scotland, appellate courts make decisions on the basis of documents, with occasional oral argumentation, while in Sweden, judges watch video-recordings of the testimony given in the first instance court, which is sometimes supplemented with new testimony.

In Italy, legal verdicts are always delivered both orally and in writing, including the court's motivations. In Sweden, verdicts are sometimes delivered orally and always in written form. In the United States and Scotland, verdicts and sentences are always delivered orally but on different occasions, and in

Scotland they are sometimes also delivered in writing in the form of sentencing statements or judgment summaries.

The different constellations of judges deliberating with other judges or lay judges, provide different interactional challenges in our different courts and national settings, which in turn generate diverse forms of frustration. While deliberations with lay judges may frustrate professional judges as a result of the lay judges' legal incompetence and their focus on 'wrong' issues, deliberations with professional colleagues actualise status differences and power struggles. The oral presentation of judgments provides a standardised outlet for what we call moral speeches to the defendant, while the written judgments in Sweden and Italy provide an outlet for expressing anger towards professional legal counsel.

Even though common law has the aim of adapting to evolving cultural changes in a more dynamic way than civil law, all types of legal systems are intrinsically influenced by their cultural contexts, and for the purpose of understanding anger, we need to situate the legal traditions within their national emotional cultures. As indicated by previous research in this field, legal emotional regimes appear to be affected by the general emotional expressiveness of specific cultures. An emotionally expressive culture allows for stronger and more articulate emotional expressions within the dispassionate legal regime (Wettergren and Bergman Blix, 2021). As demonstrated by research from the United States, an angry judge in an expressive culture may shout and gesticulate so that everyone in the courtroom gets the message (Scarduzio, 2011; Maroney, 2012), while the subdued emotional culture found in Sweden directs judges' anger in subtle ways that only a trained eye will notice, such as taking off one's glasses or putting down one's pen (Bergman Blix and Wettergren, 2016). In our material, Italy and the United States represent expressive emotional cultures (Konewko, 2016; Wouters, 2007), while Sweden and Scotland represent subdued emotional cultures (Daun, 1996; Wouters, 2007).

Method

This book draws on a large international project exploring the emotive-cognitive process of legal decision-making in Sweden, Italy, the United States, and Scotland.[3] The project is focused on judges and prosecutors in first instance and appellate courts, that is, the state employees required to form objective and impartial, that is rational, decisions. Data were collected during the period 2018–2024 via a combination of ethnographic methods: observations, interviews, and shadowing. We have shadowed prosecutors and judges

3 This research has received funding from the European Research Council (ERC) under the European Union's Horizon 2020 research and innovation programme, awarded to Bergman Blix (grant agreement No 757625).

while they prepare cases, observed them at hearings and deliberations, and interviewed them before and after hearings. In Sweden, we have conducted 90 interviews and shadowed 47 judges and 26 prosecutors working on 70 different cases. In Italy, we have conducted 95 interviews and shadowed 40 judges and 34 prosecutors working on 80 cases. In the United States, we have conducted 55 interviews and shadowed 21 judges and 25 prosecutors over 71 days, while in Scotland, as a result of our access being rescinded,[4] we have only conducted five interviews and shadowed 7 judges for 15 days during court hearings.

We have focused on cases of homicide, intimate partner violence (IPV), and fraud, but other crime types were included either as part of the charges in these cases or as part of the cases that the legal professionals were working on during the shadowing process. Since our sampled cases are often considered serious offences, the professionals in our data include an overrepresentation of experienced practitioners (indicated by age rounded down to the nearest five years, with people aged over 65 being described as 65+ for reasons of anonymity). In total, we have roughly the same number of women and men, and they are to a large extent white and middle class (with a slightly more diverse racial and class background in the United States). Overall, this reflects the demographics of judges and prosecutors in the countries examined.

During our shadowing, we followed individual judges or prosecutors during their workday, prompting them to engage in continuous reflections on their everyday practice (McDonald, 2005; Czarniawska, 2007) in between hearings and deliberations, such as during office work and breaks from hearings. During hearings and deliberations, we were silent observers and were able to take notes continuously, focusing on interactions between legal professionals and between professionals and lay people, and noting word choices, voice changes, body language, facial expressions, gestures, and glances. During the 'in-between' situations, we prompted reflections on what was about to happen or what had just happened in hearings and deliberations. These reflections were noted in retrospect and supplemented with audio-recorded interviews, which included questions about the current case and comparisons with other cases. Interviews were semi-structured, with a focus on the interactions we were observing, and were of varying length depending on the interview occasion. Interviews were recorded and transcribed in a way that took note of emotional cues such as tone of voice, pauses, and emphases. Data from all countries were coded separately and then merged into a large data set.

4 After we gained formal access to the courts and started fieldwork, the court authority step by step retracted access by prohibiting specific questions and signalling to judges who had expressed interest in the project that they should not participate, so we decided to end the fieldwork.

For the purpose of this book, we have analysed all coded instances of conflict, irritation/frustration/anger, and anger metaphors. The analysis followed an abductive process (Timmermans and Tavory, 2012) in that it moved between the data, previous research on legal anger, and theorising about anger, which involved looking at how legal professionals employ anger to steer the legal process in court and solve legal problems. This means that we have excluded instances in which legal professionals expressed anger about issues of a more general kind, such as anger at technical failures, or at work overload. In analysing expressions of anger, we used Suzanne Retzinger's (1991) concept of "angry cues", which comprise the verbal and visual markers of anger that she found when analysing American couples' marital quarrels. In the text, we mark raised voices with UPPER CASE LETTERS, and emphasised words with *italics*. Verbal markers include both anger words, such as 'mad' or 'irritated', and ways of speaking, for example in a staccato voice with multiple emphases, or with sarcasm, while visual markers may include lowered eyebrows being drawn together, pressing the lips together so that they form a straight line, or leaning forward. Verbal ("I'm so mad!"),[5] and visual ("her voice is trembling and she speaks each word with force") expressions were taken to indicate experiences of anger, which were sometimes also validated in retrospect from the participants' own accounts in follow-up interview transcripts, when participants talked about these instances.

Two additional points are important here. First, expressions of anger do not necessarily mean that people feel angry. A judge might, for example, raise his voice and lean forward towards the defendant without feeling upset in the moment; he may simply want to stop the defendant interrupting the witness during an examination. However, when sitting on the train on his way home from work, irritation might bubble up when he thinks back on the rude defendant (this particular incident was described in Bergman Blix and Wettergren, 2018: xi). These temporal dimensions of anger, and our analysis of the relations between how anger is felt and displayed in connection with work tasks and processes, are traced in Chapter 3 on *Timely temper*. Second, and on a more general note, anger, or any emotion, is made meaningful in the social situations and interactions in which it occurs. To interpret the meaning of anger, and whether and how anger influences (inter)action, we need to understand the situation (Scheff, 2000). Our extensive fieldwork in courts in the respective countries, and the detailed reflections of judges and prosecutors during shadowing and in interviews, were vital to our understanding of how situations and actions made sense to our participants, while comparisons between situations and interactions in the different cultural contexts have been vital to enable us to tease apart how sense-making is dependent on legal and emotional norms. The selection of countries, with its variations in legal

5 It was rather uncommon in our data that people said that they were angry in the moment. This type of verbal cue, if articulated, usually came when reflecting on a situation afterwards.

system factors and emotional expressiveness, turned out to be particularly important when analysing anger, and although we found a lot of similarities – legal professionals get angry in relation to roughly the same things in all four countries examined, as depicted in Chapter 2 on *Nagging narratives*, different countries stood out in unexpected ways, as we will see in particular in Chapter 4, *Respectable rage*.

References

Ambos Kai. (2003) International criminal procedure: "adversarial", "inquisitorial" or mixed? *International Criminal Law Review* 3: 1–37.

Averill James R. (1983) Studies on anger and aggression: Implications for theories of emotion. *American psychologist* 38: 1145–1160.

Bandes Susan A. (1996) Empathy, narrative, and victim impact statements. *The University of Chicago Law Review* 63: 361–412.

Bandes Susan A. (1999) *The Passions of Law*. New York: New York University Press.

Bandes Susan A. (2021) Feeling and thinking like a lawyer: Cognition, emotion, and the practice and progress of law. *Fordham Law Review* 89: 2427–2446.

Bandes Susan A and Blumenthal Jeremy A. (2012) Emotion and the law. *Annual Review of Law and Social Science* 8: 161–181.

Bandes Susan, Madeira Jody Lyneé, Temple Kathryn, et al. (2021) *Research Handbook on Law and Emotion*. Northampton, MA: Edward Elgar Publishing.

Belleau Marie-Claire, Johnson Rebecca and Bouchard Valérie. (2008) Faces of judicial anger: Answering the call. *European Journal of Legal Studies* 1: 415–458.

Bergman Blix Stina. (2022) Making independent decisions together: Rational emotions in legal adjudication. *Symbolic Interaction* 45: 50–71.

Bergman Blix Stina and Wettergren Åsa. (2016) A sociological perspective on emotions in the judiciary. *Emotion Review* 8: 32–37.

Bergman Blix Stina and Wettergren Åsa. (2018) *Professional Emotions in Court: A Sociological Perspective*. London: Routledge.

Bergman Blix Stina and Wettergren Åsa. (2019) The emotional interaction of judicial objectivity. *Oñati Socio-Legal Series* 9: 726–746.

Bergman Blix Stina and Wettergren Åsa. (2024) Integrating rationality and emotion in legal institutions. In: H Flam (ed) *Research Handbook on the Sociology of Emotion: Institutions and Emotional Rule Regimes*. Northampton, MA: Edward Elgar Publishing, 173–197.

Bitsch Anne. (2019) *Voldtektens geografi. En studie av den rettslige forvaltningen av seksuelt medborgerskap i Norge*. PhD thesis. Department of Sociology and Human Geography, University of Oslo, Oslo.

Bladini Moa. (2013) *I objektivitetens sken: en kritisk granskning av objektivitetsideal, objektivitetsanspråk och legitimeringsstrategier i diskurser om dömande i brottmål (In the semblance of objectivity - a critical review of objectivity claims and legitimation strategies in criminal trial discourses)*. Göteborg: Makadam förlag.

Bourdieu Pierre. (1986) The force of law: Toward a sociology of the juridical field. *The Hastings Law Journal* 38: 814–853.

Braithwaite John. (1989) *Crime, Shame and Reintegration*. Cambridge: Cambridge University Press.

Bright David A and Goodman-Delahunty Jane. (2006) Gruesome evidence and emotion: Anger, blame, and jury decision-making. *Law and Human Behavior* 30: 183–202.

Brunsson Karin and Brunsson Nils. (2017) *Decisions: The Complexities of Individual and Organizational Decision-Making*. Cheltenham, UK: Edward Elgar Publishing.

Burkitt Ian. (2014) *Emotions and Social Relations*. London: SAGE.
Cherry Myisha. (2021) *The Case for Rage: Why Anger Is Essential to Anti-Racist Struggle*. Oxford: Oxford University Press.
CJP. (1942) The Swedish Code of Judicial Procedure (Rättegångsbalken).
Clark Candace. (1997) *Misery and Company. Sympathy in Everyday Life*. Chicago: University of Chicago Press.
Cottingham Marci D. (2022) *Practical Feelings: Emotions as Resources in a Dynamic Social World*. Oxford: Oxford University Press.
Czarniawska Barbara. (2007) *Shadowing and Other Techniques for Doing Fieldwork in Modern Societies*. Malmö: Liber.
Dahlberg Leif. (2009) Emotional tropes in the courtroom: On representation of affect and emotion in legal court proceedings. *Nordic Theatre Studies* 21: 129–152.
Daun Åke. (1996) *The Swedish Mentality*. University Park: The Pennsylvania State University Press.
Deonna Julien A and Teroni Fabrice. (2015) Emotions as attitudes. *dialectica* 69: 293–311.
Dworkin Ronald. (1986) *Law's Empire*. Cambridge: Harvard University Press.
Feigenson Neal. (2016) Jurors' emotions and judgments of legal responsibility and blame: What does the experimental research tell us? *Emotion Review* 8: 26–31.
Fischer Agneta H and Roseman Ira J. (2007) Beat them or ban them: The characteristics and social functions of anger and contempt. *Journal of Personality and Social Psychology* 93: 103–115.
Flower Lisa. (2018) Doing loyalty: Defense lawyers' subtle dramas in the courtroom. *Journal of Contemporary Ethnography* 47: 226–254.
Flower Lisa. (2020) *Interactional Justice: The Role of Emotions in the Performance of Loyalty*. Abingdon, Oxon: Routledge.
Frijda Nico H. (1986) *The Emotions*. Cambridge: Cambridge University Press.
Garfinkel Harold. (1956) Conditions of successful degradation ceremonies. *The American Journal of Sociology* 61: 420–424.
Garland David. (1993) *Punishment and Modern Society: A Study in Social Theory*. Chicago: University of Chicago Press.
Georges Leah C, Wiener Richard L and Keller Stacie R. (2013) The angry juror: Sentencing decisions in first-degree murder. *Applied Cognitive Psychology* 27: 156–166.
Goldberg Julie H, Lerner Jennifer S and Tetlock Philip E. (1999) Rage and reason: The psychology of the intuitive prosecutor. *European Journal of Social Psychology* 29: 781–795.
Hochschild Arlie Russell. (1983) *The Managed Heart: Commercialization of Human Feeling*. Los Angeles: University of California Press.
Holmes Mary. (2004) The importance of being angry: Anger in political life. *European Journal of Social Theory* 7: 123–132.
Karstedt Susanne. (2002) Emotions and criminal justice. *Theoretical Criminology* 6: 299–317.
Keltner Dacher, Gruenfeld Deborah H. and Anderson Cameron. (2003) Power, approach, and inhibition. *Psychological Review* 110: 265–284.
Kemper Theodore D. (1978) *A Social Interaction Theory of Emotions*. New York: John Wiley & Sons.
Konewko Simonetta Milli. (2016) *Neorealism and the "New" Italy: Compassion in the Development of Italian Identity*. New York: Palgrave MacMillan.
Konradi Amanda. (1999) "I don't have to be afraid of you": Rape survivors' emotion management in court. *Symbolic Interaction* 22: 45–77.
Kusenbach Margarethe and Loseke Donileen R. (2013) Bringing the social back in: Some suggestions for the qualitative study of emotions. *Qualitative Sociology Review* 9: 20–38.

Kövecses Zoltán. (2000) *Metaphor and Emotion: Language, Culture, and Body in Human Feeling*. Cambridge: Cambridge University Press.
Leiterdorf-Shkedy Shira and Gal Tali. (2019) The sensitive prosecutor: emotional experiences of prosecutors in managing criminal proceedings. *International Journal of Law and Psychiatry* 63: 8–17.
Lerner Jennifer S and Tiedens Larissa Z. (2006) Portrait of the angry decision maker: How appraisal tendencies shape angers influence on cognition. *Journal of Behavioral Decision Making* 19: 115–137.
Lorde Audre. (1997) The uses of anger. *Women's Studies Quarterly* 25: 278–285.
Maroney Terry A. (2011) The persistent cultural script of judicial dispassion. *California Law Review* 99: 629–681.
Maroney Terry A. (2012) Angry judges. *Vanderbilt Law Review* 65: 1207–1286.
Maroney Terry A and Gross James J. (2014) The ideal of the dispassionate judge: An emotion regulation perspective. *Emotion Review* 6: 142–151.
May Allyson. (2005) Advocates and truth-seeking in the old bailey courtroom. *The Journal of Legal History* 26: 83–90.
McDonald Seonaidh. (2005) Studying actions in context: A qualitative shadowing method for organizational research. *Qualitative Research* 5: 455–473.
Miceli Maria and Castelfranchi Cristiano. (2019) Anger and its cousins. *Emotion Review* 11: 13–26.
Minissale Alessandra. (2023) *Emotions in legal decisions: The construction of objective narratives in Italian criminal trials*. PhD thesis. Department of Sociology, Uppsala University, Uppsala.
Mishra Pankaj. (2018) *Age of Anger: A History of the Present*. London: Penguin Books.
Nordquist Cecilia Y. and Bergman Blix Stina. (2022) Expanding emotional capital in court. *Frontiers in Sociology* 7: 1–12.
Nussbaum Martha C. (2016) *Anger and Forgiveness: Resentment, Generosity, Justice*. Oxford: Oxford University Press.
Parsons Talcott. (1939) The professions and social structure. *Social Forces* 17: 457–467.
Pierce Jennifer L. (1995) *Gender Trials – Emotional Life in Contemporary Law Firms*. Berkeley: University of California Press.
Quigley Brian M and Tedeschi James T. (1996) Mediating effects of blame attributions on feelings of anger. *Personality and Social Psychology Bulletin* 22: 1280–1288.
Retzinger Suzanne M. (1991) *Violent Emotions: Shame and rage in marital quarrels*. London: Sage Publications.
Roach Anleu Sharyn and Mack Kathy. (2013) Judicial authority and emotion work. *Judicial Review* 11: 329–347.
Roach Anleu Sharyn and Mack Kathy. (2017) *Performing Judicial Authority in the Lower Courts*. London: Palgrave Socio-Legal Studies.
Roach Anleu Sharyn and Mack Kathy. (2019) Impartiality and emotion in everyday judicial practice. In: R Patulny, A Bellocchi, RE Olson, K Sukhmani, JP McKenzie and M Peterie (eds) *Emotions in Late Modernity*. Abingdon: Routledge, 253–266.
Roach Anleu Sharyn and Mack Kathy. (2021) *Judging and Emotion: A Socio-legal Analysis*. Abingdon, Oxon: Routledge.
Rosa Hartmut. (2020) *The Uncontrollability of the World*. Cambridge: Polity Press.
Rosenwein Barbara H. (1998) *Anger's Past: The Social Uses of an Emotion in the Middle Ages*. Cornell: Cornell University Press.
Rosenwein Barbara H. (2020) *Anger: The Conflicted History of an Emotion*. Yale: Yale University Press.

Scarduzio Jennifer A. (2011) Maintaining order through deviance? The emotional deviance, power, and professional work of municipal court judges. *Management Communication Quarterly* 25: 283–310.
Scheff Thomas J. (2000) *Bloody Revenge: Emotions, Nationalism, and War*. Lincoln, NE: iUniverse.com.
Silva Laura. (2024) Is anger a hostile emotion? *Review of Philosophy and Psychology* 15: 383–402.
Simon Dan. (2019) On juror decision making: An empathic inquiry. *Annual Review of Law and Social Science* 15: 415–435.
Sorial Sarah. (2019) Emotions and the criminal law: Anger and the defence of provocation. In: R Patulny, AO Bellocchi, RE Olson, K Sukhmani, JP McKenzie and M Peterie (eds) *Emotions in Late Modernity*. London: Routledge, 129–141.
Spencer John R. (2016) Adversarial vs inquisitorial systems: Is there still such a difference? *The International Journal of Human Rights* 20: 601–616.
Srinivasan Amia. (2018) The aptness of anger. *Journal of Political Philosophy* 26: 123–144.
Tiedens Larissa Z and Linton Susan. (2001) Judgment under emotional certainty and uncertainty: The effects of specific emotions on information processing. *Journal of Personality and Social Psychology* 81: 973–988.
Timmermans Stefan and Tavory Iddo. (2012) Theory construction in qualitative research: From grounded theory to abductive analysis. *Sociological Theory* 30: 167–186.
Tiscione Kristen Konrad. (2019) Feelthinking like a lawyer: The role of emotion in legal reasoning and decision-making. *Wake Forest Law Review* 54: 1159–1196.
Törnqvist Nina. (2017) Att göra rätt. En studie om professionell respektabilitet, emotioner och narrativa linjer bland relationsvåldsspecialiserade åklagare (Doing just right: A study on professional respectability, emotions and narrative lines among prosecutors specialised in relationship violence). PhD thesis. Department of Criminology, Stockholm University, Stockholm.
UNODC. (2006) *The Bangalore Principles of Judicial Conduct*. United Nations Office on Drugs and Crime.
Weber Max. (1978) *Economy and Society*. Berkeley: University of California Press.
Weber Max. (1998) Bureaucracy. In: HH Gerth and CW Mills (eds) *From Max Weber: Essays in Sociology*. New York: Routledge, 196–244.
Wettergren Åsa and Bergman Blix Stina. (2021) Comparing Culturally Embedded Frames of Judicial Dispassion. In: S Bandes, JL Madeira, K Temple and E Kidd White (eds) *Research Handbook on Law and Emotion*. Northampton, MA: Edward Elgar Publishing, 146–163.
Wouters Cas. (2007) *Informalization: Manners and Emotions since 1890*. London: Sage.

2 Nagging narratives

> IT'S ONE THING for us to sit here and BELIEVE or be completely conVINCED that this person has been beaten or whatever it may be, but we have to look at what the evidence covers, BECAUSE THAT'S OUR TASK. So, YES, even if I can feel convinced myself, I try to ... push it away ... by leaning towards 'But what does the evidence say?', because that's what's crucial. Then, of course, I want right and correct rulings, so I don't want to sit [frustrated] and acquit when I feel convinced that ... someone has done something. But ... but it will ultimately be up to the evidence to make that judgement, anything else would be unreasonable [end frustrated]. So yes, I can probably feel a lot but I ... I probably don't make much of it.
>
> Judge Amanda, 30+, appellate court,
> post-hearing interview, murder, Sweden

In an interview after handling a murder trial, Judge Amanda raises her voice, emphasises many words and speaks with an engaged tone; she is frustrated and angry (cf. Retzinger, 1991). The reason for her anger is that she cannot convict a defendant whom she "feels convinced" is guilty. But Judge Amanda distances herself distinctly from her upset feelings by differentiating between what has happened in the case, the truth, and what can be proved in court. She hints at a gap between on the one hand her intuition and common sense, her 'gut feelings' (cf. Minissale, 2024), and on the other a notion of juridical relevance based on the high standards required when evaluating evidence. The narratives she hears in court may nag her to convict, but she needs to resist this urge. This separation of truth from legal evaluation illustrates professional boundary at work (Lamont and Molnár, 2002), with Judge Amanda emphasising the importance of legal expertise, as illustrated by her description of having to remind lay judges to focus on the evidence, since they tend to take the wrong route, by starting at what they perceive to be the truth. In a legal sense, a crime has been committed when the necessary prerequisites are met, and it can be proven 'beyond reasonable doubt'. In practice, this means that in court hearings 'what really happened' may be of subordinate importance, and the process of legal evaluation can be both

DOI: 10.4324/9781003330592-2

puzzling and alien to someone who is not acquainted with legal practice, such as a lay judge or jury member.

Judge Amanda's boundary work is interesting because she appears to link interpretation and intuition to evaluating the truth ("I UNDERSTAND that this person has DONE THIS"), whereas legal evaluations and assessment instead appear to lie beyond interpretative evaluation. By taking herself out of the equation, making the evidence itself the active agent ("it will ultimately be up to the evidence to make that judgement"), her feelings and thinking play no part in interpreting and evaluating the evidence (cf. Bladini, 2013). She can *feel* that a person is guilty, but her job is not to feel, it is to apply the law to facts. In contrast with Judge Amanda's depiction, research in philosophy and psychology has over recent decades highlighted the way in which emotions are important drivers in epistemic processes, both motivating and monitoring lines of inquiry and also promoting salience and directing attention (de Sousa, 2009; Morton, 2010; Arango-Muñoz and Michaelian, 2014; Muis et al., 2018). As we have shown elsewhere (Bergman Blix and Minissale, 2022; Bergman Blix, 2022; Törnqvist and Wettergren, 2023; Bergman Blix and Törnqvist, 2024), the acquisition of legal knowledge is no exception; epistemic emotions such as curiosity, doubt, and certainty are essential components of legal decision-making. While we do not intend to designate anger as an epistemic emotion, since in fact, anger is commonly regarded as "non-epistemic" (Morton, 2010: 25) and is known to distort epistemic activities (Wild, 2016: 133), we feel it is crucial to understand how anger, irritation, and frustration operate in "epistemically related contexts" (Muis et al., 2018: 169), such as the legal setting. The unsettling character of anger as a nagging emotion makes it a common part of epistemic processes. Brun and Kuenzle (2008: 16) maintain that "[e]motions kick in when we are cognitively challenged, when our knowledge seems false, inadequate, irrelevant or not useful" and in this chapter we want to both narrow and broaden this claim – narrowing it by focusing on the discrete emotion of anger, while at the same time broadening it by scrutinising the social dynamics of fact finding and legal encoding, which are areas in the scholarship of law and emotion that still remain unexplored and elusive.

In this chapter we tend to what legal professionals get angry about in court. We show that anger becomes a tool to delineate legal relevance and to counter perceived inefficiency, manipulation or unfairness and thus underscores central values for the legal process as such. Importantly, the anger logic in court differs from the presumed logic of anger in everyday life. Going back to Judge Amanda, her frustration and anger are linked to her predicament of not being able to act on her feelings ("I can probably feel a lot but I … I probably don't make much of it."). Anger that results from 'knowing' a person is guilty but not being able to act on this by convicting them is an intuitively logical form of anger. But in a legal setting, this is not the accepted logic of anger. Instead, legal anger commonly sets out to encourage narratives that are suited to legal evaluations and assessments. Indistinct narratives pose challenges for legal professionals in various ways, but they are nevertheless important to connect 'what really happened' to the legal world. In other words, the legal form itself invites a complex interpretation and translation process between the 'real' and the legal sphere, which is reliant on legal rationality, comparisons, and common sense. Building on Tilly (2008), we conceptualise this process and its associated set of practices as *legal encoding*. Legal encoding is an epistemic process and, as will be shown, irritation and anger can serve as emotional tools for signalling inefficiency, confusion, or unfairness. As we show in the first section, anger – when it functions as a guide to collecting and evaluating stories in court – often balances between constraining stories to make them fit for legal evaluation and being dependent on credible stories that tend to remain messy.

Irritation as tool of the trade – unruly lay stories

One common source of irritation among legal professionals relates to the fact that the way people talk about events and motivate their actions in everyday life is very different from what is expected in court (Tilly, 2008). While lay people's testimonies often serve as important evidence, legal anger is used to *restrain* an overly elaborate telling of the 'true' story in court (Bergman Blix and Minissale, 2022). In all of the countries in our study, judges and prosecutors commonly became frustrated when the testimony of a defendant, plaintiff, or witness was too long, covering not only various aspects of the criminal event but also introducing details that had little or no legal relevance for the case at hand. In this section, we explore the irritation that judges and prosecutors describe in relation to lay people whose narratives do not follow the script for what the legal professionals consider a proper account, for example because they are too lengthy, unclear, or unfocused.

In everyday accounts, people often give a cause and effect explanation for their actions (I could not pay my rent because I lost my job), and they thus need to contextualise their activities to clarify situations and incentives (Tilly, 2008). In court, however, these elaborated narratives can lead legal professionals to lose sight of information that might relate to the relevant legal prerequisites.[1] For prosecutors, who need to engage in transforming the messy reality of witness statements and other pieces of information into a well-defined indictment, truth is a complicated issue (Wettergren and Bergman Blix, 2016). During the trial, prosecutors need to present reliable and credible witness statements and, to some extent, lay narratives that are perceived as being credible or true are disorderly. In an interview conducted

1 Although legal evaluations of criminal activities build on intent, this should not be confused with motive. Intent refers to the 'mens rea' (guilty mind) of the defendant who intended to do something that the law determines to be wrong (Moore, 2011). Legal encoding refers to fitting activities into relevant codes, and not about linking motives to actions.

during a murder trial in Italy, Prosecutor Francesco (30+) reflected on this inherent conflict.

> This witness is a very particular witness [serious tone], also not collaborative. Many times she made me, the court, angry. It wasn't easy to listen to her...she's a free spirit [laughs] who didn't want to be there. The data is: she said certain things, overall. *ACTUALLY,* she didn't [slow pace] say those things, let's say, *against* someone, but this can even be *positive* in the evaluation of [faster pace] the credibility of the witness. Because, *actually*, she's not a person moved by hostility against anyone, and she told those facts in a neutral way. Also because, *afterwards*, she didn't care about them, *after all.* She didn't have a specific *interest*, a *rivalry*, or so on [sighs].
>
> Prosecutor Francesco, 30+, first instance court, post-hearing interview, murder, Italy

During the hearing, Prosecutor Francesco repeatedly expressed his frustration at this witness, who "got on his nerves" by not respecting the legal procedure's call for succinct answers, both for reasons of efficiency and the need to reflect a clear story line (Felstiner et al., 1980). In the quotation above, however, Prosecutor Francesco also reflects on the fact that the witness's legal unruliness may constitute an advantage in relation to the evaluation of her credibility. Her lack of "rivalry" and persistence in not taking a stance against anyone made her story less clear, but perhaps also truer in the sense of being more credible. While her way of speaking got on his nerves, it might be to his advantage in proving his case, and in retrospect, he expresses respect for her "free spirit". In this case, Prosecutor Francesco did not manage his irritation during his examination of the witness, but in retrospect he evaluated her "unruliness" as important for the legal evaluation of her testimony.

However, meandering narratives do not always convey credibility. In a case focused on drugs sales, Judge Erik (50+, Sweden) instead spoke about a growing confusion, as one of the police witnesses, seemingly in an effort to be objective and avoid expressing a personal point of view, had instead become incomprehensible. The witness was commenting on a video clip in which the defendant appeared to take (what was later shown to be) drugs from a van, and the prosecutor asked him whether the defendant did indeed have something in his hand. When Judge Erik saw the surveillance video, he "got the *impression*" that the man was fetching a package, but he needed the police witness's first-hand observation to turn this impression into a fact:

> ...but when asked whether he did actually leave with the drugs, the witness expressed himself extremely vaguely and could NEVER answer yes or no: 'have you seen?' Yes or no. It's just [mimics] 'I got the impression' and 'I had the impression that' [end mimicry] and so on... And I

mean that's not the same as having seen it. No, no. And it's very, very strange, and he seemed to be under the impression that it was the same thing. Eh, and then you become, because in that case he has a very strange idea of language, right? You just can't make it out.

Judge Erik, 50+, first instance court, post-hearing interview, drug trafficking, Sweden

In contrast to Judge Erik's impression of a somewhat distant and blurred video film, the police witness had been standing in close proximity to the actual event, but he refrained from answering yes or no to rudimentary factual questions – did you or did you not see the man leaving with a package? The witness separated what had actually happened from what he had seen with his own eyes ("I got the impression"). In this way, he was presumably trying to be exact (his eyes interpreted what he saw as a man leaving with a package), but Judge Erik instead thought the witness was confusing the issue with "a very strange idea of language", turning a simple fact into a metaphysical conundrum. In the end, the witness's way of expressing himself forced Judge Erik to make interpretations of which he was not completely certain, generating a nagging frustration. Indistinct and vague formulations chafe against the demands for exactitude and preciseness in the context of legal language and legal assessments. In this example, the incoherence in the witness's narrative was further amplified by his wordy testimony with cumbersome details, which in the view of the judge made it strange and peculiar.

As can be seen from the above examples, muddied and indistinct answers and incoherent narratives tend to elicit irritation and frustration. However, overly specific answers also constitute a source of irascible emotions. In a backstage area following a court hearing, Prosecutor Andrea (60+, Italy) sarcastically slandered a witness in the following way:

This witness [a bar owner] has a great memory. I'm pleased for him. *Well done*! [sarcastic tone] (...) However, he doesn't convince me. You know, he's *too* precise. Was he working that afternoon, or was he looking at the defendant? [slams his hands down hard on the piece of paper]

Prosecutor Andrea, 60+, first instance court, post-hearing interview, IPV, Italy

Prosecutor Andrea's indignation also became apparent in the way he started to speak in dialect (cf. Williams et al., 2020) and, although he was joking, his voice was tinged with seriousness. His assessment of the witness's credibility ends dismissively ("he doesn't convince me") and his indignant emotions appear to be anchored in scepticism and a distrust of the witness. A combination of common-sense assumptions about memory and the work situation of bartenders here resulted in a belief that the witness was dishonest and not telling the truth. This finding is in line with previous research showing that actions that are perceived as tampering with the truth elicit irritation, for example when lay people are perceived as lying (Maroney, 2012) or when victims are reluctant to provide the same information that they gave during a police interrogation when testifying in court (Törnqvist and Wettergren, 2023). These studies illustrate not only that the legal process and obtaining justice are heavily reliant on oral evidence and on lay people's narratives, but also that legal professionals are emotionally invested in this reliance. This investment makes them prone to defend their preliminary evaluations, and thus opens up for anger when lay people do not live up to these expectations. Furthermore, it explains why anger is often absent in hearings involving recidivist offenders, who know how to navigate the interaction order of the courtroom, and to a greater extent align their answers to professional expectations.

In the epistemic process of understanding lay narratives, irritation signals legal irrelevance, which poses a threat to both evaluation and efficiency, and also a need to be careful not to let the feeling of irritation get the upper hand over objectivity, as indicated by Prosecutor Francesco's ambivalent stance in assessing the witness's credibility. If it is acknowledged and managed, irritation may lead to rigour in deciding whether a story should be cut short or whether it is instead important to continue listening. In an interview with Judge Debora (45+, Italy) about cases involving intimate partner violence, she linked irritation to testimony that covered a time frame that was unnecessarily long and that included details of emotional rather than abusive aspects, but she also stressed the importance of being thorough before cutting these stories short:

> I *OFTEN* see that, when the defendant or the witness victim is interviewed, they start from the GREEK CALENDS! [annoyed tone] They give a series of details about their marriage that to me have a relevance that is, I have to say, quite limited. It is obvious that to them from a sentimental, emotional point of view, maybe the fact that the husband has not bought a birthday present is a *big deal* [annoyed tone]. eh... Here, I mean, the line between a relationship *facing a crisis, A PATHOLOGICAL ONE,* [slower] and *abuse* is a very fine one that nevertheless needs to be traced.
>
> Judge Debora, 45+, post-hearing interview,
> first instance court, IPV, Italy

Judge Debora's irritation emerges from the discrepancy between the narrow legal interest in the abusive acts that meet the legal requirements of the case at hand, and those aspects of the relationship that the involved parties attach great importance to, and her irritation is paralleled by disinterest (see also Törnqvist, 2017). While Judge Debora's irritation marks a division between abuse in a legal sense and the victim's experience of "a crisis", her crossness also seems to invite empathic reflection, as she speaks more slowly and acknowledges that "the line between a relationship *facing a crisis, a pathological one* and *abuse* is a very fine one". Drawing the line between relevant and irrelevant information is not straightforward, but it is a line that "nevertheless needs to be traced", and it makes the demarcation of stories a tricky job, both for the people giving testimony and the professionals who are in charge of guiding the storytelling and evaluating its relevance.

The examples from Judges Debora and Eric, and Prosecutors Francesco and Andrea, illustrate the narrow line that lay people need to walk in order to present a legally relevant and credible story in court – neither overly certain and succinct, nor overly uncertain and expansive. Legal professional irritation thus serves to signal a need for demarcation as well as a potential need for emotion management in order not to jeopardise the elaborations that are needed to be able to evaluate relevance and credibility.

Enforcing compliance

Irritation and anger at lay people's disorderly narratives are common in all the countries represented in our data. When lay people talked about the 'wrong things', in the 'wrong ways' and at the 'wrong time', anger was used as capital to enforce conformity (Nordquist and Bergman Blix, 2022), but procedural rules structure and steer irritation at lay people's unruly narratives in different ways. One significant difference between the common law and civil law systems relates to the possibility that legal professionals have to prepare witnesses prior to the court hearing. While prosecutors in Sweden and Italy are reluctant to meet victims or witnesses as a trial approach, since this is viewed as a breach of the objectivity principle, prosecutors in the American (and to some extent Scottish) legal contexts are expected to prepare witnesses for a court hearing. When shadowing Prosecutor Tess (30+, USA) after a preliminary hearing in an aggravated robbery and homicide case, she reflected on the performance of a police witness. As in the drug case described by Judge Erik above, this police witness had been called to comment on a video recording of the event in question, and Prosecutor Tess was not happy with his testimony:

> Terrible! *SO BAD!* You can tell that he needs to be prepped not to say what he thinks... [sighs] He's not very seasoned so I should have worked with him beforehand. [annoyed tone] He could be accused of having given his personal opinion. He was very combative and he was arrogant.
>
> Prosecutor Tess, 30+, first instance court, post-hearing interview, robbery and homicide, USA

Prosecutor Tess's annoyance includes a small degree of self-regret ("I should have worked with him beforehand") but a major part of her anger and blame is directed at the witness, and not herself. Her frustration with this witness resonates with two immanent ideals for witnesses' performances in court, the one of which builds on general emotional rules about cooperativeness and humility ("He was very combative, and he was arrogant"), while the other relates to the procedural rules of common law systems regarding the presentation of evidence ("He could be accused of having given his personal opinion"). Tess's annoyance emanates from an interactional expectation of civility, which ensures the smooth running of the court hearing, and a fundamental legal notion about how truth and justice is best obtained. The strict regulation of the way evidence should be presented in US courts requires advanced emotional work, since prosecutors need to be attentive to objections from the judge and defence lawyers while at the same time assisting victims and witnesses in telling their stories. During the court hearing referred to above, the defence lawyer had objected several times when the witness commented on the defendant's intentions ("here he is getting ready to commit the robbery"). On one occasion, the judge had sustained the objection and Tess had turned to the witness and said, "just explain what you can see without speculation", putting her hand out and sounding annoyed. Prosecutor Tess's display of annoyance served as a rule reminder to the police witness, who should have known the rules of the court, to account only for the facts of the case and not his evaluation of the defendant's intentions.

While such rebukes are common in the United States and Scotland, Italy and Sweden both operate a freedom of evidence principle, and the involved parties are asked to start by providing their unrestricted stories of the criminal event. While legal professionals, and defence lawyers in particular, may stress that there should be no speculation, different forms of interpretation and opinions are tolerated to a much greater extent in Sweden and Italy. This does not mean that legal professionals in these countries do not use outbursts of irritation as a means of attempting to guide witnesses. In the extract below, Judge Oscar (60+, Italy) repeatedly becomes angry and sarcastic towards the witness in a murder case that was widely reported in the public media, telling her not only how to talk but also how she should understand the questions being posed to her:

> VICTIM COUNSEL: ... but have you ever talked to the defendant, saying 'have you heard that on TV.... They said that I might have done that', have you?
>
> WITNESS: Nope ...this morning I do not remember that.
>
> JUDGE OSCAR: So this *morning no*, but maybe tomorrow *yes*. But we are here *today*.
>
> Witness tries to interrupt.
>
> JUDGE OSCAR: You mustn't interrupt, you are not letting us finish the questions, you gave your answer immediately, YOU MUST NOT DO THAT, OTHERWISE THE MENTAL PROCESS (processo mentale) IS THAT YOU ALREADY HAVE THE ANSWER, AND THAT YOU'RE NOT INTERESTED [slow pace, keeps shouting] IN THE QUESTION.

Contrary to that, we would like you to listen to the question, and to not engage in any mental process *DURING* the question. The question is: there were TV programmes on that continuously, has your boyfriend talked to you about them?

WITNESS: I already answered before, I said I don't remember.

Judge Oscar, 60+, first instance court,
fieldnotes hearing, murder, Italy

In this extract, Judge Oscar intervenes in the examination of the victim counsel when he perceives the witness to be disrespecting the court ("this morning I do not remember that") and rebukes the witness by mimicking her sarcasm ("So this *morning no*, but maybe tomorrow *yes*."). He identifies the problem with her answers being that they are ready-made ("THE MENTAL PROCESS IS THAT YOU ALREADY HAVE THE ANSWER"). His angry outburst then shifts into a calmer instruction whereby he, in a way similar to Prosecutor Tess above ("just explain what you can see without speculation"), tries to coach the witness's testimony ("listen to the question, and do not engage in any mental process DURING the question"). Just as Prosecutor Tess's instructions were linked to procedural rules, Judge Oscar's efforts to get the witness to "listen to the question" are linked to the procedural principles of orality and immediacy, which require evidence to be presented verbally in court (the court does not read case files prior to trial). In both these cases, irritation and anger are used to attempt to enforce compliance and respect for the court, but with limited success.

As illustrated by Judge Oscar above, judges sometimes assist prosecutors and counsels when the question-and-answer ritual gets out of hand, thus engaging in teamwork (Goffman, 1959). In one case in Scotland, for example, Judge Mackenzie (50+, Scotland) interrupted the prosecutor's examination of a witness, saying, "Ms. [name of the prosecutor] was very clear to you to answer the questions asked", and when the witness continued in the same vein, Judge Mackenzie sighed and raised her shoulders, saying, "There are rules in this court and they need to be *followed*!". A similar example but more expressive form of irritation was seen in an American case, where two witnesses were talking at the same time, and were talking about facts that the court viewed as irrelevant. Judge Nathania (50+, USA) interrupted, putting her hand up as a signal to stop saying:

"I do not wanna hear about his stuff." At this point, the witness's son tries to speak up and Judge Nathania and the court officer both raise their voices and says, "HOLD ON!" The son continues to develop his point, but judge Nathania jumps in again and says "Y'ALL! I get your point, but it still remains, *who cares*!".

Judge Nathania, 50+, first instance court,
fieldnotes hearing, IPV, USA

In this last example, several procedural rules are broken: the witnesses speak at the same time, when only one of them is giving evidence, and they speak on issues that the court does not want to hear about at this specific point in the hearing. Judge Mackenzie and Judge Nathania both try to get the witnesses to stick to the procedural rules, but the witnesses do not wish to follow them or do not understand what the rules require. The rebukes made in US courts stand out in the sense that judges at times use more informal language in a way that was not seen in the other countries ("Y'ALL", "*who cares!*" etc).

Failed interactions often result in impatience and irritation that goes beyond what the legal professionals regard as acceptable. Asked whether she ever felt that an emotion had limited her ability to perform well professionally, Prosecutor Agata (45+, Sweden) started speaking about direct examination and cross-examination of lay people, saying that:

> In the end, I can get pig-headed and irritated. And then I can feel that was no good. When you leave [the situation], I feel that 'you could have had more patience'. Particularly during the examination, that's when you get angry. [...] You become irascible. And that's stupid; that's not professional. You should have ignored that comment; that was unnecessary.
>
> Prosecutor Agata, 45+, interview, Sweden

As this quote illustrates, prosecutors become irritated and frustrated when their quest for knowledge lingers in limbo. This frustration is related to their professional commitment to understand what has happened, and obstacles to this knowledge-seeking process tend to elicit hostile emotions. Due to the principles of orality and immediacy, the quality of the judges' decisions is dependent on the ability of the legal professionals to ensure the quality of the oral evidence presented to the court. The irritation of prosecutors in such situations is thus entangled with their professional pride at being able to secure robust and valid legal decisions. At the same time, in the above quote Prosecutor Agata describes regretting her displays of sullenness or acidic comments, since these interfere with the politeness and calmness expected of legal professionals in the courtroom (Roach Anleu and Mack, 2021). In the asymmetrical power hierarchy of the courts, legal professionals are expected to restrain their anger to not risk exceeding the scope of their authority (Kemper, 1978). In our data from Sweden, patience is a common counter-emotion used by legal actors to control, or at least tone down, their anger and irritation when lay people speak too much about legally irrelevant matters or too little about legally relevant matters.

In all these examples, the legitimation for irritation and anger is found in an ambition to maintain the interactional order of the courtroom, and specifically to manage the presentation of narratives that are lacking in stringency, efficiency, and timing. Legal principles (such as orality and immediacy) and procedural rules (such as evidentiary regulations) provide a framework for the interactional order that directs outbursts of anger in different directions depending on legal system. In this way, anger protects against harm to certain core legal values while risking harm to others, such as procedural fairness and the right to be heard. This kind of anger is shared by legal professionals in court. For judges, a parallel type of anger is generated when *other legal professionals* do not keep to the boundaries of what the court considers relevant.

Confusing legal argumentation – interprofessional anger

Legal encoding is facilitated by narratives and legal arguments that are organised and presented in a legally efficient way. Judges across the different jurisdictions expressed irritation with narratives that they perceived to be "scattered", "messy", "sloppy", or evasive in some other sense. In a similar vein, judges often made a powerful point of their preference for closing arguments that are "short and concise", and that focus on the 'real' legal issues, rather than the lengthy and unclear argumentation that legal professionals may engage in before the court. Scattered and unclear reasoning serves as an obstacle to the epistemic aims of judges during court proceedings (Muis et al., 2018: 169), and results in anger, frustration, and irritation. In Italy, a common way of speaking about this obstacle was to say that the legal argumentations "got on their nerves", hinting at the irritation and anxiety involved. An Italian Judge, Sara (50+) expressed frustration with lawyers who put "too much meat on the fire" (tanta carne sul fuoco), implying that defence lawyers sometimes deliberately create confusion by presenting a massive, and by extension, messy, narrative. Another common metaphor focused on questions and queries "weighing down" court proceedings, a metaphor that was used by both prosecutors and judges to describe court cases in which superfluous information slows down, and complicates, the knowledge-seeking process. Deviations from 'pure' legal arguments, and narratives that are contaminated with irrelevant details, elicited sparks of irritation in all of the countries included in the research.

While prosecutors and defence lawyers enact different legal positions and therefore face different expectations, failures by both types of legal professionals to maintain a tight narrative are a common ground for irritation among judges. In a fraud case in Sweden, Judge Josef (50+) expressed frustration with the defence lawyer in the case, who had "used a shotgun when he should have had a precision weapon", explaining that the many objections raised by the defence lawyer actually ended up contradicting one another. Moreover, since some of the matters the defence lawyer had called into question related to minor details of no real consequence for the outcome of the case, Judge Josef said, "I'm not saying that he's done that work without due cause, but the issues related to details of specific charges, about where purchases have been made or [mobile phone] mast positionings here or there, they are of lesser value". Expanding on this line of thought, Josef also noted that "all those details could have been spared, and then you would imagine that it might also have been a few hundred thousand Swedish Crowns cheaper". Here we can surmise that one underlying reason for Judge Josef's irritation may be found in "reasons of the state" (Weber, 1998), which involve an obligation to be economical with the state's resources (cf. Törnqvist and Wettergren, 2023).

We do not have data from defence lawyers, but from a prosecutorial perspective, prosecutors' rationale to "keep hammering in" complex evidence, can be an attempt to make, for example, technically complicated evidence obvious, even "boring" (Prosecutor Linus, 35+, fraud, Sweden) to prove their case. For the prosecutors, at least in Sweden and Italy, it does not appear to be evident where the line goes between what the court will regard as being over-zealous and what the court will view as constituting a sufficient amount of information to get the ruling they are hoping to obtain.

When Judge Josef was asked whether the defence lawyer's performance affected Josef's trust in him, he said:

> It is rather that maybe the patience … That my patience with certain questions that he asked became … Well, in the end, you might think that … You sigh a little. And then maybe, in the end you don't take the objections seriously. And that's maybe not trust in the person, but trust in the material that you're trying to highlight.
>
> Judge Josef, 50+, first instance court, post-hearing interview, fraud, Sweden

This quote exemplifies the close links between irritation and impatience. Judge Josef's reflection also suggests that information that is deemed to be irrelevant risks tainting the judge's view of the reliability of information that is presented subsequently. Irrelevant information may thus damage a judge's trust in the material as a whole. As a concluding comment, and echoing the views of several other legal professionals in our data, Judge Josef recommended that all legal parties at a trial should make wise decisions about which issues to contend. Referring to another aspect of the same type of behaviour, a judge we shadowed in a court of first instance in the United States, Judge Blake (60+) loudly commented that:

> IF YOU'RE GOING TO *SIT* AND *FIGHT* AND *PICK* ABOUT EVERY LITTLE THING AND JUST BE A THORN, YOU'RE PROBABLY NOT DOING MUCH FOR YOUR CLIENT; [harsh tone] you're just putting on a show for yourself and it can hamper [bangs desk] the way the case is handled. You may not get everything that you would normally get.
>
> Judge Blake, 60+, first instance court, fieldnotes hearing, IPV, USA

According to judge Blake's understanding, long-winded objections may come across as vanity and selfishness, neither helping the client nor the case but instead being interpreted as showing unprofessional conceit. In a similar vein, Italian Judge Aurora (50+) spoke of becoming irritated at prosecutors and defence lawyers who do not get to the point and related her irritation to her work burden and the need for efficiency. Talking about the prosecutor in an intimate partner violence case, Judge Aurora described the prosecutor as "excessively meticulous" and noted in an annoyed tone that the prosecutor focused on details that did not "have much weight in the matter". Developing her thoughts, Judge Aurora went on to describe the aspects of the case that she thought were of legal relevance. She then said that "having *so many trials*, and so much to do" made her think that:

> For *all* trials in my opinion, to go for the *ESSENTIAL*. [...] I would have ... [laughter] I would not say, get irritated, but the excessive insistence on *INSIGNIFICANT* details ... even the dates, whether it is the 2nd, or the 3rd, makes *ABSOLUTELY NO DIFFERENCE*. [...] But in a case like this, in which the violence or conduct occurred *REGULARLY*, whether the injury was on January 2nd, or 3rd, or 4th [irritated tone of voice] *NOTHING CHANGES* [slowed pronunciation]. [...] Habituality interests me ... *FREQUENCY* and also *THE DURATION* of the conduct, there is a difference between two months and two years... But whether an event happened one day or two days later, this does not, I repeat, unless there is a *compatibility* issue with other circumstances.
>
> Judge Aurora, 50+, first instance court,
> post-hearing interview, IPV, Italy

In this quote, we can see that Judge Aurora's irritation navigates between interest and disinterest, dismissing the significance of certain aspects of the abuse, such as specific dates, while emphasising the importance of habituality, frequency, and duration to being able to understand and evaluate the criminal acts.[2] The quotes from Judge Aurora and Judge Josef illustrate our finding that the judges' irritation with massive narratives often becomes amplified by further criminal legal procedural rationales, such as demands for cost and time efficiency. Together, these examples illustrate the irritation felt by judges at information that is perceived as "inadequate, irrelevant, or not useful" (Brun and Kuenzle, 2008: 16), and that in effect gets in the way of

2 For intimate partner violence cases in Italy, habitualness is an important prerequisite. The occurrence of regular abuse over an extended period tones down the importance of individual dates. In contrast, in Sweden habitualness is demonstrated by selecting incidents of abuse that have occurred on several (more than two) individual dates and corroborating each of these incidents with supporting evidence.

being able to identify and dissect the material that is essential for their legal encoding process.

Angry clarifications, anxious hints

Separating the (legally) relevant from the (legally) irrelevant lies at the core of legal encoding practices, and irritation in these instances relates to the way the amount of information presented slows down the epistemic process of legal professionals. While the irritation triggered by messy narratives presented by other legal professionals serves as an obstacle to the legal encoding process in all countries, the different countries' varying interaction orders affect the routes taken by this irritation, and how it manifests itself. In the two common law countries included in our study, Scotland and the United States, judges are rather overt and direct in communicating their frustration at prosecutors' and defence lawyers' deficiencies in presenting a coherent and legally compelling narrative. In these two contexts, judges can give their views on the relevance of the legal arguments directly in the courtroom, allowing frequent interruptions to the interaction order when they perceive the legal arguments to be inadequate. To illustrate this dynamic, we turn to a court proceeding in a US court of appeal. This case was handled by a panel of three judges, and we direct our focus at one of these, Judge Frederick (50+):

> Judge Frederick turns to the defence lawyer: "*Again*, what does that have to do with *absconding* ...?". Judge Frederick asks the question with more emphasis this time. The defence lawyer says, "It doesn't... that's a decision for the trial court ..." Judge Frederick replies, "*Well* ... that has been the bulk of your argument ... *absconding* ... *kicked out*... How is that *relevant* to this *at all*?" Judge Frederick now sounds slightly annoyed. The defence lawyer tries to repair the situation and answers, "I think we are saying the same thing but missing each other ..."
>
> Judge Frederick, 50+, appellate court, fieldnotes
> hearing, revocation of probation, USA

In this sequence, we see Judge Frederick asking straightforward questions about the relevance of the defence lawyer's main narrative and not hesitating to call the defence lawyer's legal argumentation into question. In this way, Judge Frederick gives the defence lawyer a chance to substantiate his arguments further, and while Judge Frederick's irritation demonstrates his having a different view, it does not involve a strong confrontation. At the same time, Judge Frederick makes no attempt to hide his irritation with the defence counsel, and in our American and Scottish data, we find several displays of authoritarian, unapologetic irritation, such as when Judge Ewan (60+, Scotland) reproached a prosecutor for struggling to formulate a question: "Maybe if you pause and think about what you want to say before you pose the question". The prosecutor quickly signalled submissiveness: "I'll do that, my lord."

As a comparison, we turn to the Swedish legal context, in which judges seldom interrupt prosecutors or defence lawyers in this interrogative manner. While Swedish judges may ask for clarifications of the legal reasoning, they more commonly give 'hints' about how other legal actors should change their argumentation (see Judge Konrad in Chapter 3). Even though both prosecutors and defence lawyers are receptive to these 'hints' during court proceedings, misunderstandings commonly spark irritation in Swedish courtrooms, among both judges, prosecutors, and defence lawyers (Bergman Blix and Wettergren, 2019). In the following quote, we meet Judge Irene (50+, Sweden), who was speaking about her overall impression of the defence lawyer in a murder case. First, she acknowledged that the defence lawyer did not have an easy task, since the defendant's aim was to be completely acquitted, despite there being strong evidence in the case. She continued:

> I think maybe the closing argument FELL SHORT, because it was scattered [laughs] a little bit all over the place and I wasn't really able to keep up. With some kind of stringency there [unclear feeling] ... Perhaps it [the closing argument] was more confusing than it was clarificatory. That is my opinion of the defence lawyer's contribution [lowered voice]. [...] And then he was talking about issues that I didn't really think were important in the sense that it wasn't anything that was a big deal in the case itself. [...] Like, *when* the defendant had DECIDED to murder the victim. [...] And what is the *motive*, and then he talked about homosexuality or - and it's nothing that has become a big deal in the case, so it was like 'Well, what does that matter THEN [annoyed]?' [...] That's more confusing than helpful to me understanding things [Lowered voice].
>
> Judge Irene, 50+, appellate court, post-hearing interview, murder, Sweden

The varying pitch and emphasis in this quote suggest that Irene is critical of the defence lawyer's performance. However, her anger seems rather mild, with the deficiencies in the closing argument being elucidated with laughter and hesitancy. The object of Irene's anger, however, is specified (as was the case with Judge Frederick) and is due to the absence of coherence in the lawyer's arguments, which instead of facilitating Irene's legal encoding and assessment of the case, leave her more confused. Since there was little room for Judge Irene to resolve this confusion during the defence lawyer's closing arguments (by asking elucidatory questions, like Judge Frederick, or by slapping down the other legal professional in the way Judge Ewan did), Judge Irene used laughter to diminish the importance of the issue, and throughout this interview segment, Irene's anger bordered on disappointment and resignation (cf. Thagard, 2008: 168), an emotional dynamic that is more prominent in the Swedish data than in that from the other countries.

One interesting difference between the countries examined is that in the common law countries, the United States and Scotland, the judges articulated what they viewed as problematic aspects of the other legal professionals' legal presentations and used irritation to guide these other professionals in what they perceived to be the preferred direction. In contrast, judges in the civil law countries believed that such explicit directives would risk their impartiality, which led to displays of irritation being expressed as hints that might be difficult for the recipient prosecutors to understand.

Twisting evidence and trust issues

In the courtroom, prosecutors and defence lawyers often play out an antagonistic relationship, in which competing narratives about 'what really happened', or contradictory legal assessments, constitute a central dimension (Flower, 2020). From the prosecutors' perspective, the alternative accounts presented by defence lawyers incite both interest and irritation, an emotional nexus that is related to challenges of one's certainty, status, and professional honesty. Sometimes in expected ways, sometimes in startling ways, the defence introduces narratives that nag and chafe. As we will show in this section, this kind of irritation is informed by an underlying game of trust, focused on who can and who cannot be trusted in the courtroom. In the following sequence we will meet Prosecutor Louise (50+, Sweden), an experienced prosecutor, who in this instance was dealing with a case of attempted murder. Overall, throughout the trial, there were good prospects that Louise's indictment would result in a guilty verdict and at the end of the trial Louise was confident and proud over the way she was handling this complex case at trial. Nonetheless, the defence lawyer was still able to stir up uncertainty and irritation with her closing argument on the last day in court. Closing arguments are the phase of the trial when both defence lawyers and prosecutors present their narrative in its entirety, often in an emotionally charged way, bringing points of disagreement to a head as we will see in the following extract from the trial when the defence lawyer questions the whole basis of the prosecution:

> In her closing argument, the defence lawyer self-assuredly states that there are "many crimes that the prosecutor does not even mention" in her account of the case. Hearing this, Prosecutor Louise leans slightly forward over her desk, a gesture that hints at both attentiveness and irritation. The defence lawyer goes on, questioning whether two of the witnesses in fact should be seen as accomplices instead of witnesses. At this point, Prosecutor Louise sighs deeply. With some sharpness in her voice, the defence lawyer concludes by stating that "I *understand* that the prosecutor has disregarded all of this because *she needs* witnesses and not accomplices. But the plaintiff could just as well be seen as a

co-defendant". Throughout this part of the defence lawyer's closing argument, Prosecutor Louise shifts between looking sternly at the defence lawyer, down at her papers and directing short glances towards the judges.

Prosecutor Louise, 50+, first instance court, fieldnotes hearing, attempted murder, Sweden

There are several layers of hostile emotions at play in this interaction. Not only had the defence lawyer introduced a completely different narrative of the events at issue, using a soft, rather easy-going tone (as if her argument was nothing special), she was also implying harsh criticism of the preliminary investigation. As a part of the game of trust, directing her arguments at the prosecutor in particular, the defence lawyer was suggesting that Prosecutor Louise had been sloppy and selective in the way she had presented the course of events. In addition, to strengthen her own case and diminish the court's trust in the prosecutor, the defence lawyer was painting a picture of the prosecutor as consciously having omitted potential co-defendants and accomplices.

Since impartiality and meticulousness are core values in the work of prosecutors, these criticisms can be interpreted as face-threatening acts (Goffman, 1967; Bloch, 2012) and as an attempt to damage Prosecutor Louise's trustworthiness and status in the courtroom. Aggressive actions of this kind may be viewed as a form of professional ambush, and in our data such attacks elicited anger among prosecutors, and they constitute one of the situations in which airing irritation and protest during the court proceedings is often perceived as appropriate by Swedish prosecutors (Wettergren and Bergman Blix, 2016). Importantly, the defence lawyer was not only undermining the prosecution's narrative, but also the prosecutor as a narrator ("because she *needs* witnesses and not accomplices"), thus breaking a taken-for-granted trust in the prosecutor as a professional. In other words, the defence lawyer's arguments incorporated a meta-narrative about the prosecutor's narrative being twisted and unreliable. In the subtle ways required by the interactional order of the Swedish courtroom, Prosecutor Louise responded to the defence lawyers' chastisement by means of a mixture of attention and disinterest (similar to defence lawyers' performances of dramatic reductions, see Flower, 2020), but also by demonstrating irritation.

In the break after the defence lawyer's closing argument, Prosecutor Louise dismissed the defence's claims as being "far-fetched" and contrary to common sense, but the argument had also stirred a nagging worry about how it would affect the judges' ruling. In an interview a few days later, Prosecutor Louise said that while she thought the defence lawyer's rhetoric was "clever" and "striking", she also thought it was "exaggerated". By means of ridicule and mockery, Prosecutor Louise manifested both that her status remained intact and confidence in her way of presenting the course of events associated with the crime. Prosecutors expect counter-narratives from defence lawyers and anticipate struggles over 'what really happened'. Prosecutor Louise's anger in this case was instead linked to threats to her trustworthiness and professional status, illustrating that the line between fair play and foul play in the courtroom is a thin one. Showing distrust constitutes a form of social power that embodies moral criticism (Hawley, 2017). In this particular case, the defence lawyer undermined Prosecutor Louise's competence as well as her sincerity.

In another example of irritation and twisted narratives, we would like to address situations in which legal professionals perceive that another legal actor is using personal and private allusions in the courtroom. As we saw in the above case involving Prosecutor Louise, this irritation may relate to situations in which the legal actors' private person is used to both discredit their professional status and challenge their trustworthiness. At the other end of the spectrum, alluding to the personal may also be viewed as an attempt to flatter another legal professional. When the actor in question sees through such attempts, they are usually openly dismissed, as was the case with the Scottish Judge, Fiona (70+), when a defence lawyer tried to ingratiate himself by emphasising Judge Fiona's long experience. Judge Fiona immediately responded in an irritated tone, saying, "Leave my experience out of it!", thus creating a sharp line of demarcation against irrelevant argumentation. In another short excerpt from a US courtroom, Judge Blake (60+) rebuked a defence lawyer who was trying to push for a dismissal:

> In this case, the witness is not present, so Prosecutor Iris says she is going to postpone it for six months. The defence lawyer then stands and says, "My hope was to get this dismissed today." Judge Blake tilts his head and says in a slightly sarcastic tone, "I hate to spoil your hope, but how can I make a judicial decision to dismiss a case without hearing both sides of the story… So you want me to give him special treatment?" His voice is sarcastic. The defence lawyer walks up to the podium and says in a cheerful tone, "Yes sir, I want you to give all my clients special treatment," and they all laugh.
>
> Judge Blake, 60+, first instance court, fieldnotes hearing, IPV, USA

The defence lawyer in this case expressed his disappointment at the postponement of the case, insinuating that bad prosecutorial management or a disorganised court were to blame, in order to effectuate a favourable outcome for his client. Judge Blake then challenged his attempt to twist the process by responding with sarcasm, and the defence lawyer quickly saved face by making a joke of his request. These attempts at manipulation elicit irritation from judges, and in these instances irritation may serve as a protection against being deceived by unreliable information and twisted narratives.

Previous research has suggested that court proceedings may be seen as "sympathy contests" (Kusenbach and Loseke, 2013) in which prosecutors, defence lawyers, and victims' counsels try to influence judges to favour their clients by using "sympathy cues" (Törnqvist, 2022). Speaking of the two defence lawyers in a murder trial in Italy, Judge Ines (40+) stated that they were "really good" but also said that "one almost wanted to move me to pity, sometimes it bothers me when they do it too much … a little tear-jerking, but he did say something legally relevant …". In another example from our Italian data, which relates to a case of manslaughter, Judge Bianca (30+) complained about the inclusion of photos of the murdered person in her file. Judge Bianca said that she does not understand the purpose of showing her these photos: "He's dead anyway… that is, if it is a deliberate attempt to murder, the photos can make sense to highlight aspects that are relevant from a legal perspective, but this way it makes no sense". Judge Bianca continued, saying that the photos made her feel a deep sadness and that this sadness led her to wonder why these photos had been shown to her in this way, instead of being stored digitally, so that they could be consulted if necessary.

The question of how juries are affected by gruesome evidence has been thoroughly discussed in previous research (Bright and Goodman-Delahunty, 2006; Bandes and Salerno, 2014) and in the data from the United States, there are judges who talk about how they remove photos in murder cases in order to not "inflame" the jury and affect their decision-making in a prejudicial way. In Sweden, where the evaluation of evidence is free, considerations of this kind are not possible. However, the court administration tends to choose experienced lay judges for trials involving murder and sexual violence. On the basis of Judge Ines' and Judge Bianca's experiences, sympathy appears to put judges on their guard by eliciting annoyance and irritation. These feelings of irritation create distance and an ability to review and scrutinise narratives or evidence that is perceived as being twisted by means of emotional manipulation. The combination of irritation and sympathy produces mistrust and suspiciousness towards the legal professional, sometimes in the form of a brief and circumscribed doubt, sometimes in the form of lingering feelings of wariness.

As we have seen, the issue of who to believe in court relates not only to lay people, such as defendants, victims, and witnesses, but also to prosecutors and defence lawyers. While credibility is pivotal when evaluating the narratives of lay people, the narratives of legal professionals are also related to various games of trust. To trust is to take a risk, but some level of trust is nonetheless required to move forward (Barbalet, 2019). Trust plays out differently to the different legal professionals. For prosecutors, some narratives nag because they introduce a new angle, shaking the prosecutors' trust in their own evaluation. Here, anger is directed at themselves, and gives rise to a need to attend to and scrutinise their earlier assessments, such as when Prosecutor Louise briefly questioned her indictment in the attempted murder case. Other narratives nag because they twist and distort what the prosecutors believe to be true and real about the criminal incident in question. This anger stems from legal pathos, an ambition to get things right. Yet other narratives nag because they portray the prosecutor as being unreliable, unprofessional, or not objective. Here, anger is directed at the opposing party, but is also tinged with professional shame, as a result of being accused of insincerity and incompetence (cf. Hawley, 2017). For prosecutors, twisted narratives are part of the adversarial process and are often managed by using anger and distance as a means of securing one's status and self-confidence. For judges, who preside over the process, they need to manage direct attempts to twist narratives in order to affect their evaluations by means of outright anger and dismissal. An underlying emotional current in judges' work deals with the question of who, and what information, to trust and not to trust.

References

Arango-Muñoz Santiago and Michaelian Kourken. (2014) Epistemic feelings, epistemic emotions: Review and introduction to the focus section. *Philosophical Inquiries* 2: 97–122.

Bandes Susan A and Salerno Jessica M. (2014) Emotion, proof and prejudice: The cognitive science of gruesome photos and victim impact statements. *Arizona State Law Journal* 46: 1003–1056.

Barbalet Jack. (2019) The experience of trust: Its content and basis. In: S Masamichi (ed) *Trust in Contemporary Society*. Leiden: Brill, 11–30.

Bergman Blix Stina. (2022) Making independent decisions together: Rational emotions in legal adjudication. *Symbolic Interaction* 45: 50–71.

Bergman Blix Stina and Minissale Alessandra. (2022) (Dis)passionate law stories: The emotional processes of encoding narratives in court. *Journal of Law and Society* 49: 245–262.

Bergman Blix Stina and Törnqvist Nina. (2024) Navigating uncertainty and negotiating trust in judicial deliberations. *Frontier in Sociology* 9: 1–11.

Bergman Blix Stina and Wettergren Åsa. (2019) The Emotional Interaction of Judicial Objectivity. *Oñati Socio-Legal Series* 9: 726–746.

Bladini Moa. (2013) *I objektivitetens sken: en kritisk granskning av objektivitetsideal, objektivitetsanspråk och legitimeringsstrategier i diskurser om dömande i brottmål (In the semblance of objectivity - a critical review of objectivity claims and legitimation strategies in criminal trial discourses)*. Göteborg: Makadam förlag.

Bloch Charlotte. (2012) How do perpetrators experience bullying at the workplace? *International Journal of Work Organisation and Emotion* 5: 159–177.

Bright David A and Goodman-Delahunty Jane. (2006) Gruesome evidence and emotion: Anger, blame, and jury decision-making. *Law and Human Behavior* 30: 183–202.

Brun Georg and Kuenzle Dominique. (2008) Introduction: A new role for emotions in Epistemology? In: G Brun, U Doguoglu and D Kuenzle (eds) *Epistemology and Emotions*. Aldershot: Ashgate, 1–31.

de Sousa Ronald. (2009) Epistemic feelings. *Mind and Matter* 7: 139–161.

Felstiner William LF, Abel Richard L and Sarat Austin. (1980) The Emergence and Transformation of Disputes: Naming, Blaming, Claiming. *Law and Society Review* 15: 631–654.

Flower Lisa. (2020) *Interactional Justice: The Role of Emotions in the Performance of Loyalty*. Abingdon, Oxon: Routledge.

Goffman Erving. (1959) *The Presentation of Self in Everyday Life*. New York: Doubleday.

Goffman Erving. (1967) *Interaction Ritual. Essays on Face-to-Face Behavior*. New York: Pantheon Books.

Hawley Katherine. (2017) Trust, distrust, and epistemic injustice. In: IJ Kidd, J Medina and G Pohlhaus (eds) *The Routledge Handbook of Epistemic Injustice*. Abingdon: Routledge, 69–78.

Kemper Theodore D. (1978) *A Social Interaction Theory of Emotions*. New York: John Wiley & Sons.

Kusenbach Margarethe and Loseke Donileen R. (2013) Bringing the social back in: Some suggestions for the qualitative study of emotions. *Qualitative Sociology Review* 9: 20–38.

Lamont Michèle and Molnár Virág. (2002) The study of boundaries in the social sciences. *Annual Review of Sociology* 28: 167–195.

Maroney Terry A. (2012) Angry Judges. *Vanderbilt Law Review* 65: 1207–1286.

Minissale Alessandra. (2024) Scrutinizing Gut Feelings: Emotional Reflexive Practices in Italian Courts. *Emotions and Society* 6: 7–25.

Moore MS. (2011) Intention as a marker of moral culpability and legal punishability. In: RA Duff and S Green (eds) *Philosophical Foundations of Criminal Law*. Oxford: Oxford University Press, 179–204.

Morton Adam. (2010) Epistemic emotions. In: P Goldie (ed) *The Oxford Handbook of Philosophy of Emotion*. Oxford: Oxford University Press, 385–399.

Muis Krista R, Chevrier Marianne and Singh Cara A. (2018) The role of epistemic emotions in personal epistemology and self-regulated learning. *Educational Psychologist* 53: 165–184.

Nordquist Cecilia Y. and Bergman Blix Stina. (2022) Expanding emotional capital in court. *Frontiers in Sociology* 7: 1–12.

Retzinger Suzanne M. (1991) *Violent Emotions: Shame and rage in marital quarrels*. London: Sage Publications.

Roach Anleu Sharyn and Mack Kathy. (2021) *Judging and Emotion: A Socio-legal Analysis*. Abingdon, Oxon: Routledge.

Thagard Paul. (2008) How cognition meets emotion: beliefs, desires and feelings as neural activity. In: G Brun, U Doguoglu and D Kuenzle (eds) *Epistemology and Emotions*. Aldershot: Ashgate, 167–184.

Tilly Charles. (2008) *Why?*. Princeton: Princeton University Press.

Törnqvist Nina. (2017) Att göra rätt. En studie om professionell respektabilitet, emotioner och narrativa linjer bland relationsvåldsspecialiserade åklagare (Doing just right: A study on professional respectability, emotions and narrative lines among prosecutors specialised in relationship violence). PhD thesis. Department of Criminology, Stockholm University, Stockholm.

Törnqvist Nina. (2022) Drizzling sympathy: Ideal victims and flows of sympathy in Swedish courts. *International Review of Victimology* 28: 263–285.

Törnqvist Nina and Wettergren Åsa. (2023) Epistemic emotions in prosecutorial decision-making. *Journal of Law and Society* 50: 208–230.

Weber Max. (1998) Bureaucracy. In: HH Gerth and CW Mills (eds) *From Max Weber: Essays in Sociology*. New York: Routledge, 196–244.

Wettergren Åsa and Bergman Blix Stina. (2016) Empathy and objectivity in the legal process: The case of Swedish prosecutors. *Journal of Scandinavian Studies in Criminology and Crime Prevention* 17: 19–35.

Wild Markus. (2016) Critical reflections on affective epistemology. In: G Brun, U Doguoglu and D Kuenzle (eds) *Epistemology and Emotions*. Aldershot: Ashgate, 125–147.

Williams Aya, Srinivasan Mahesh, Liu Chang, et al. (2020) Why do bilinguals code-switch when emotional? Insights from immigrant parent–child interactions. *Emotion* 20: 830–841.

3 Timely temper

Emotions are often depicted as volatile phenomena, as momentary immersions in the present that permeate the body and the mind. As we saw in the introduction, anger is emblematic of this idea of emotions, connoting short, explosive, and intense sensations, metaphorically depicted as a "pressurised container" (Kövecses, 2009: 386). In this chapter, we will problematise this understanding of emotions as solely ephemeral matters and explore legal anger from a temporal perspective. We demonstrate how legal anger builds over time, interacts with other emotions, and comes in different degrees of intensity and duration; we delve into the temporal alignment of anger with professional work in court.

In the previous chapter, we looked at *what* legal professionals get angry about in court. In this chapter we look at *how* anger is intertwined with the interaction order of the courtroom. Moving between frontstage arenas, such as the courtroom and public parts of the courthouse, and backstage offices and meeting rooms, we can see how anger adapts both temporally and spatially to different tasks and ideals (Goffman, 1959). In some instances, anger is not acted upon, or even felt, in direct connection with the frontstage interaction in which it originates, but is postponed while solving the problem that induced the anger to begin with. Anger can then be expressed as short and intense outbursts backstage (Bergman Blix and Wettergren, 2018: xi), and can simmer as a low key energiser frontstage. Towards lay people, anger is often balanced with courtesy (Scarduzio, 2011; Roach Anleu and Mack, 2021); a swift moving in and out of anger in order to emphasise the seriousness of the situation without jeopardising institutional and relational trust. Sometimes however, it is not that easy to let go of anger, and it spreads across situations, particularly towards other legal professionals, when the reason for anger needs to remain unarticulated. In these situations, anger can signal diminished confidence and anxiety about how to manage the case, and in the longer term may develop into stale resentment towards a particular occupational group, such as the police or defence lawyers.

DOI: 10.4324/9781003330592-3

Anger at work

One common way of scrutinising anger, and also the patterns of other emotions in social life, is by looking at the norms, or feeling rules for *when* emotions are considered appropriate or inappropriate in particular situations and relations, as well as their *duration* and *intensity* (Hochschild, 1983). Anger, which often signifies an inappropriate emotion, becomes 'foregrounded' in our mind as intense and disruptive (Barbalet, 2009; Barbalet, 2011). We notice that we are angry and that we want to act on our anger, for example, by shouting at the person who made us angry. At the same time we can feel that we should not have become angry in that situation and that acting on our anger would make us look bad or out of control. There is a discrepancy between how we feel and how we think we should feel. In these instances, we can try to manage our anger, either by *surface acting*, displaying for example a 'neutral' stone face to cover up our felt emotions, or *deep acting*, making an effort to put ourselves in the appropriate mood, for example, by taking deep breaths (Hochschild, 1983). But anger does not always alert our attention; it can stay "backgrounded" (Barbalet, 2009; Barbalet, 2011), as a low-intensity grudge. In everyday life we develop strategies for how to express and manage our anger in line with the situations we encounter, and these at-first deliberate efforts become habituated and may even go unnoticed (Bergman Blix, 2015).

From an overall perspective, western legal systems share the feeling rule that anger should not be part of professional expressions in court, but what this implies differs between different legal traditions and emotional cultures. In the following quote, Judge Tommaso (55+, Italy) reflects on his proneness to become angry in court and the expectations that different legal professionals face:

> JUDGE TOMMASO: Well, one of my flaws is that the lawyers tend to get on my nerves … even today, sometimes, I have given two or three pricks [reprimands], but to the lawyers. Sometimes I tend to be a bit like that … […]
>
> INTERVIEWER: Are there situations in your work that lead you sometimes to lose control more?
>
> JUDGE TOMMASO: Yeah [confident tone], for sure. In the trial court, I would get pissed off much more [than in his current position as a preliminary hearings judge]. It's easy there [laughs]. Now I try to control myself much more. The hearings are shorter, anyway … anyway I hold back.
>
> INTERVIEWER: And you are aware, you realize it?
>
> JUDGE TOMMASO: Absolutely yes, absolutely yes! In fact, every now and then I compliment myself [laughs]: 'I was good at keeping myself in

> check.' Because it's not me. But, you understand, you are the judge; you are not the prosecutor. The prosecutor might have some excesses, but it is a part he plays. Theoretically, THEY ARE NOT acceptable from the judge. Going over the top is not acceptable. So, I CONTAIN MYSELF. It's self-restraint, basically.
>
> Judge Tommaso, 55+, first instance court, post-hearing interview, Italy

This quote illustrates common perceptions among legal professionals about anger in court, but it also gives us some clues into variations in anger in different countries. In all of the countries we have examined, anger, in particular for judges, is an unacceptable emotion ("one of my flaws"), that needs to be contained ("I was good at keeping myself in check"). Judge Tommaso also addresses how the roles of legal professionals provide different amounts of leeway for anger. Prosecutors may express anger ("some excesses") as part of their accusatorial role in court proceedings ("it is the part he plays"); but at least 'theoretically', it is not equally appropriate for a judge to show these emotions. Legal anger demands skilled emotion work, and these demands vary with the situation and the location. As Judge Tommaso's quote shows, he lost his temper far more often during the ritualistic interactions in trial court than he does in his current position as a preliminary hearing judge, where interactions take the form of meetings and a large part of his decisions are made on the basis of documents. In the interview, Judge Tommaso assured us that, "Anyone can see [when he gets angry]" and this reflects our court observations in Italy, the United States and Scotland, but not in Sweden (see also Maroney, 2012; Wettergren and Bergman Blix, 2021). While Judge Tommaso from Italy can describe his anger as a 'personal trait' and his management of his anger as "self-restraint basically", the same easy-going approach would not be accepted among Swedish judges.

In Sweden, judges and prosecutors distance themselves from being angry while acknowledging that they can get irritated. Swedish courts have strong norms of professional dispassion (Bergman Blix and Wettergren, 2016; Flower, 2020), and the association between anger and expressive gestures and behaviours makes this particularly problematic. In contrast to anger, *irritation* is understood to be less intense, since it "simmers" rather than explodes (Landweer, 2020: 443), and for Swedish legal professionals, the association between irritation and remaining in control ("simmering") signals cognitive rather than affectual involvement. Conceptually, irritation can also imply a mood that lacks a clear target (which emotions have); people tend to be irritated at the social environment in general rather than at a specific person or harm (Landweer, 2020). As we will see, however, for Swedish legal professionals, irritation often has a clear target, indicating that the feeling stands for what legal professionals in the other countries would call anger. The reference to irritation then becomes a way of being able to talk about anger without breaking with the strong feeling rules to suppress emotions, as illustrated by Judge Ellinor (30+, Sweden): "That is something you are taught early on, and that I totally agree with, you should not get upset. It seldom serves any purpose". The high threshold for anger to pass as appropriate in a Swedish court is thus related to the impersonal and formally correct interaction order, in which the stone-faced legal professional is paramount (Bergman Blix and Wettergren, 2016). A common way used by judges and prosecutors to detach themselves from anger is a self-narrative in which they have matured in their professional work, and as Judge Naomi (50+, Sweden) said, "It is a feeling that I have grown out of". In these self-presentations, anger is associated with inexperience and failure, pointing to the low status of anger among Swedish legal professionals.

When Swedish legal professionals admit to having been angry, they often express guilt. Asked about when she has failed to manage her anger, Judge Britta (45+, Sweden) pondered for a while and then said that there are times when she "has been on the verge" of getting angry at legal professionals who she thinks are not doing their job: "Then it sometimes slips… I remember the feeling in my body that sometimes I've probably been a little too acidic, that I've said something that's actually a bit mean, because I eventually get tired and then I push a little, and I *always* regret it". Here, Judge Britta's anger verges on contempt. Contempt and spite connote disrespectful behaviour and are viewed as inappropriate emotions as they relate to a questionable use of the asymmetrical power dynamics that exist between legal professionals and lay people in court (Maroney, 2012) or, as in this case, between the higher status judge and other legal professionals who are dependent on the judge's decisions. Developing her thoughts about regretting these instances, Judge Britta said that it depended on when her anger occurs during the court proceedings, thus highlighting the importance of the timing of legal anger. In Britta's view, acidity was most likely to "slip out" at the end of the trial, when she has lowered her guard. This was the worst possible timing for anger, since Britta said that that was the point in a trial at which it was most difficult to put things right and recreate a respectful interaction. If it happens earlier on in a trial, she could back down and say something nice as a means of trying to compensate for her acidic outburst or excusing herself. At the same time, Judge Britta's anger is rational in that it links to the interaction order of the courtroom, which demands that the respective professions assume their role-related responsibilities if the proceedings are to run smoothly. While Sweden stands out in its stark distancing from anger, the legitimate reasons for legal anger are to a large extent similar across the countries represented in our data (cf. Wettergren and Bergman Blix, 2021). The task of disliking actions that the law has determined to be morally reprehensible, while at the same time distancing oneself from decisions based on moral anger, places substantial demands on the temporality of anger. To be perceived as rational, anger not only needs to be felt for the right reason, but also to be in alignment with situational expectations and to promote sensibly energetic rather than disruptive actions.

One problem with the notions of feeling rules and foregrounded emotions is their emphasis on the emotions per se – we notice that we are angry and try to manage our anger. But feelings often flit between awareness and unawareness, making their management a partial response to a more complex phenomenon (Holmes, 2004), and rules are not always followed. As indicated by Judge Tommaso above, high-status legal professionals can often express anger despite norms requiring dispassion and get away with it (see Scarduzio, 2011 on privileged emotional deviance). Our aim in this chapter is instead to show how situations and tasks direct and shape legal professional anger. It is not primarily the feeling itself that is managed, but the situational orientation that shapes the way anger evolves.

Postponing anger

The first important adaptation of professional anger in court involves a separation between the angering event and the feeling and expression of anger. On several occasions in our data, a judge or prosecutor who has shown no, or very little, anger during the proceedings enters their office or an empty hallway and bursts out in anger. The postponing of emotionality serves to preserve the solemnity and impartiality of the courtroom (Roach Anleu and Mack, 2021), but most importantly, anger is parked out of the way in order to solve the immediate problem.

Looking more closely at the strategy of delaying anger, we trace the evolution of Judge Giorgio's (65+, Italy) anger at the unexpected introduction of a new piece of evidence during the final replies at the closing stage of a trial. Legal proceedings incorporate expectations of a certain pre-determined temporal unfolding, and when this temporality is violated it triggers anger. However, anger also abides by procedural expectations. Below, we follow Judge Giorgio in court, when the defence lawyer asks to introduce new evidence during his closing statement in a rape trial in the appellate court, in his chambers directly after this angering event, and then in his chambers again, after the trial has finished for the day. In Italy, the oral phase from opening statements to final replies is called *contradditotio* (the contradictory).

Hearing

As soon as we start, the defence asks to produce some papers, which are the transcription of the last hearing in the separate trial against defendant 2 [still at the first instance level], and a psychiatric report about the victim. Judge Giorgio raises his eyebrows in a surprised look, and immediately invites the lawyer to stop. He asks the other lawyers whether they have anything to say in reply to the closing statements given during the last hearing. No one replies. The judges move to the council chamber.

Deliberation

Judge Giorgio is very angry. As soon as he enters the council chamber, he kicks the door to close it and says that the closing statements were finished, so the defence cannot produce further documents. "Now the contradictory is screwed, FUCK! We have to let them reply to that. But the discussion is closed, SHIT!" The three judges in the panel, Giorgio, Flavia, and Michela all start searching for precedents about the introduction of new documents in a trial and finally conclude that it is not allowed at this point.

Post-hearing

At 6 pm, when we've finished all the hearings, we move back to the council chamber to pick up our stuff. Judge Giorgio comments on the behaviour of the defence lawyer [passionate tone]: "He's not loyal; he's incorrect. *I* am the one who directs the hearing; *I* am the one who gives the floor [to people]!"

JUDGE FLAVIA: You got angry, didn't you?

JUDGE GIORGIO: He's [the defence lawyer] a good one, but he's really insidious.

JUDGE FLAVIA: "You did really good!" She compliments Judge Gorgio for his way of stopping the defence lawyer immediately, giving the floor to the other lawyers for their replies. In this way, he could say that the discussion was closed and avoid the documents being produced. Otherwise, the trial would have been postponed.

Chief Judge Giorgio, 65+, Judge Flavia, 60+,
appellate court, rape, Italy

As discussed in the chapter on nagging narratives, a common source of legal professional anger is when new information enters the process unexpectedly or at the wrong time. In this extract, the defence lawyer's call apparently catches presiding Judge Giorgio off guard ("raises his eyebrows in a surprised look"), but he is an experienced judge and immediately stops the lawyer in order to gain time to sort it out. In most everyday situations, we cannot press pause. We need to resolve unexpected developments on the spot, in action so to speak. In court, the strict procedural regulations demand the continuous evaluation not only of the matter that is under scrutiny but also of the when and how of what is being presented. This can break the ordinary temporal rhythm of the unfolding interaction, suddenly bringing it to a halt. In this way, court proceedings are similar to theatre rehearsals (rather than performances), where the director can stop the actors mid-scene to ponder about how to continue. In this particular 'scene', Judge Giorgio understands that the lawyer's request will have serious implications for the continuation of the trial and whether it will finish on schedule, but he cannot decide to decline the request on the spot, since the defence lawyer might have the legal right to mess up his schedule. Anger is not a suitable response at this point, and Judge Giorgio shows no sign of feeling that he was 'about to explode' in the courtroom. But the judge does not only postpone his anger, he also has the power to pause the situation that caused his anger.

Some time later, when he has kicked the door to the chambers closed, he blows up ("Now the contradictory is screwed, FUCK! We have to let them reply to that. But the discussion is closed, SHIT!"). Now that his focus has shifted from how to solve the immediate situation of stopping the trial, and he has moved to a backstage region to solve the problem itself, he can afford to let off some steam. This explosive anger is brief, and not shared by his fellow judges, who instead start to search for relevant legal documents. His own angry energy soon zooms in on finding a solution. Both in court and in chambers, his emotive-cognitive focus is directed at the immediate here-and-now. This happened, how can we solve this in a legally correct way? His feeling of surprise alarm at the need to pause, and his anger indicate the severity of the disruption, and initiate his drive to find a solution.

It is only after the trial, when all the immediate issues have been dealt with, that the judge allows himself to admit that the target of his anger also includes the status disruption produced by the lawyer's request ("He's not loyal; he's incorrect. *I* am the one who directs the hearing; *I* am the one who gives the floor!"). Anger can feel more or less disruptive depending on the situation, but also depending on the relative status of the person expressing anger. This is because anger itself is an indicator of social status. When a high-status person such as a judge does not feel respected, this tends to evoke anger (Kemper, 1978), and high-status judges can afford to express their anger despite the ideal of unemotional justice (Scarduzio, 2011), since anger is assessed differently depending on status. High-status anger is more likely to be evaluated as proportionate and linked to an angering event, while low-status anger risks being deemed disproportionate and associated with (an emotional) personality (Bogosavljevic and Kilty, 2021; Wingfield, 2010; Shields, 2002). Judge Giorgio's status anger is intermingled with and managed by his paying respect to the lawyer's professional skill ("He's [the defence lawyer] a good one, but he's really insidious"). In court, and particularly for judges, legal brilliance is an admired quality, and at this point Judge Giorgio tones down his anger by admitting that the defence lawyer's attempt to introduce the new documents was a smart move. By giving the defence lawyer status, he also gives him some credit and the right to interrupt in the way he did; it was rude, and too late to be successful from a legal perspective, but also smart (cf. Prosecutor Louise's response in the previous chapter, page 37). As through a prism, different facets of anger become illuminated when this episode is followed over time and across different situations, even though the angering incident remains the same.

Both lawyers and judges are high-status professionals, but at this point we also need to point to the gender differences in the situation described above.[1] Both Judge Giorgio and the defence lawyer are men, whereas the two other judges in the panel were women. As we saw both during the deliberation and after the hearing, Judge Giorgio was the only one of the judges who expressed anger, although he only did it backstage. This is perfectly reasonable in this situation, since he was the presiding judge. Nor do we lack female legal professionals who express anger in our material, even though previous research has shown that high-status women who express anger risk being dismissed as unfeminine and "bitchy" (Traister, 2023; Stollznow, 2024). All legal professionals have both high status and executive power in their work and as such are likely to both feel entitled to get angry, and to get away with being angry (Scarduzio, 2011). Nevertheless, when it comes to managing others' anger, women seem to take responsibility in ways that men do not. Judge Flavia's complimenting Judge Giorgio ("You did really good!") for his way of stopping the defence lawyer is one common way of boosting male confidence in order to tone down anger and create a supportive collective environment (see also Bergman Blix, 2022 for a Swedish example). In short, it is not only important to follow the different facets of anger over time and across different situations, but also to zoom out and examine the way the social implications of anger depend on one's situational position as well as the larger cultural and relational context.

Surprise and anger

Because the legal process involves detailed rules on how to collect, process, and evaluate information, it creates high expectations of regularity, and thus inherent surprise when these rules are not met (Zerubavel, 1985: 23). Lay people regularly fail to show up when they should, act in unexpected ways, and say unexpected things, and legal professionals do not always behave in accordance with professional expectations, making surprise an ordinary part of proceedings (Bergman Blix and Wettergren, 2018: 98). Judge Giorgio's anger was linked to surprise over the defence lawyer's unexpected request to introduce new documents, and we will now look more closely at how surprise, defined as "a reaction to the sudden discovery of unexpected knowledge" (Scott, 2021: 191), can pave the way for anger, and how the intensity and duration of anger varies depending on the situation and focus, from intense and short explosions to a low-intensity energy over a longer period of time.

1 Research has shown that the race and ethnicity of legal professionals are also linked to clear differences in their ability to express emotions in general and anger in particular (Wingfield, 2010; Wingfield, 2021; Pierce, 2003). However, our sample includes too few people who are either non-white or do not share the dominant ethnicity of their respective countries to enable us to conduct such analyses.

In the following episode, we encounter Prosecutor Göran (35+, Sweden), whose anger arose out of unwelcome feelings of surprise and confusion when he encountered several problems during a fraud trial in a court of the first instance. In the courtroom, Prosecutor Göran showed no sign of anger, but during a short break in the proceedings his anger became strong in intensity but short in duration, and then simmered in the background as an energiser in his efforts to save both the prosecution and his professional face. This episode stands out in our data from Sweden, as Göran displays his anger very directly and strongly, although in a semi-secluded backstage arena:

> When Prosecutor Göran calls a witness to testify about identifying the defendant in a photo lineup, it turns out that the prosecution has called the wrong person. Prosecutor Göran appears slightly surprised and a little confused. He keeps flipping through his papers as if he is stuck and asks the witness several times if she indeed had not been called to do the photo lineup. The next problem occurs when the following witness, who had indeed been at a photo lineup, gives her testimony. The prosecutor refers to the defendant being identified in photo number six, but the defence lawyer interrupts and asks why the police report refers to photo number three. Prosecutor Göran starts looking through his papers silently and eventually says with a calm and neutral voice, "I have not seen that before. I'll have to leave it open." During the defence lawyer's cross-examination Göran keeps leafing through his papers quite loudly for a short while, then sits back and looks over at the defence. After two more examinations the judge asks whether the prosecutor has anything else to add. Prosecutor Göran replies in a calm voice, "No, but I would like to take a short break." The judge agrees and when the judge has announced a recess, Göran walks quickly out of the courtroom. Entering the hallway, he runs to an empty niche a bit further away, picks up his phone and starts dialling the number to the police. While he is waiting to get through, he opens his folder and turns to the page showing pictures of the suspect. Looking at the researcher, he says, "There have been two gigantic torpedoes in this case, but I will at least see if I can solve one of them." He continues saying that he has never had a case where a person says that she did not attend a photo confrontation. He emphasizes that he has never heard of anything like it before. Prosecutor Göran says, "If the witness is not lying", which he asserts that he does not believe, the police must have written it down wrong, although the documentation states that they had checked ID. Prosecutor Göran shakes his head and sighs.
>
> Prosecutor Göran, 35+, first instance court,
> fieldnotes hearing/break, fraud, Sweden

In this first encounter with Prosecutor Göran in court, he shows clear but subtle signs of surprise and confusion. As van Oorschot (2021: 121) has noted, legal thinking is "a materially mediated activity" that is dependent on the physical case file, and in this interaction, Prosecutor Göran seemed to 'get stuck' in his papers and repeated his questions to the witness although she had been confident and clear in her replies. In the hallway during the break he tried to understand what had happened and aired potential explanations for the witness's answer ("If the witness is not lying"), but ends up with the most probable explanation being that the police had mismatched the names of the witnesses who were called. One surprise, although a rare one (he had "never heard of anything like it before"), is not unusual, but when the next problem – the discrepancy over the numbering of the photos – turns up, Göran demonstrates his surprise a little more openly by loudly flicking through his papers.

Surprise is linked to changes in external conditions (Scott, 2021: 195), something or someone else has induced the change, which do not necessarily reflect badly on the surprised person, but two incidents of surprise one after the other risk turning into embarrassment (cf. Goffman, 1956), since it signals that the prosecutor might not have as good a grasp on the evidence as he should. Subtly demonstrating his surprise thus serves to emphasise that this information has not been provided in his documents and is thus a complete surprise to him, and nothing he should be blamed for. By magnifying his surprise, Prosecutor Göran counterintuitively gains more control since, of the two, surprise is better than professional embarrassment (Goffman, 1972; Flower, 2018). We can also note that he does not try to clarify what is going on to the court, nor indicate that he will try to solve the problem, and the judge does not ask any questions. Surprises amount to disruptions to the expected interaction order that need to be managed, but the high demands to follow prescribed procedures and form well-grounded decisions tend to make legal professionals appear passive in the face of surprises, or as in the example of Judge Giorgio above, lead them to simply stop the proceedings in order to create time to think it through. This is because surprises interrupt the expected course of events and demand a new perspective: "the interrupted agent is no longer immersed and unreflexive, nor yet poised and self-composed" (Scott, 2021: 196). Surprises threaten the prosecutor's status as a reliable bearer of information during court proceedings (Törnqvist and Wettergren, 2023) and the prosecutor does not want to risk being regarded as a person who dithers or presents ill-conceived solutions. The judge knows this and plays along by showing nothing to give the prosecutor time to repair the situation.

Frontstage, one can get the impression that nothing has happened to seriously threaten the prosecutor's case (and face). But Prosecutor Göran's fast retreat from the courtroom and running (!) in the hallway constitutes a swift change from his seemingly calm demeanour during the hearing. At this point, an angering motivation appears to 'move him forward'; he wants to confront the police who seem to have caused the mix-ups and risked his loss of face during the trial. As described in the introduction, anger relates to blame and, in this instance, a drive towards the person he blames for having lost face in court and for putting the case at risk.

> Prosecutor Göran finally gets to talk with the police officer who has conducted the photo confrontation. As they start talking, Göran moves franticly in circles and, in a rather cumbersome way asks if the police officer has time to talk, if the officer can open a case file on his computer and then what page he should look at in the preliminary investigation. Prosecutor Göran continues to ask about the number on a photograph in the photo confrontation, saying that in all of the other cases there has been another number. All of a sudden Prosecutor Göran aims his foot at the concrete wall in front of him and kicks it hard. The kick apparently hurts his foot, and he jumps on one leg for a short while and yells "OUCH!". He then continues to talk with the police officer over the phone as if nothing has happened. Before ending the call, he says, "Don't do this again" in a cold yet neutral tone. As the researcher looks over at Prosecutor Göran, he says "He just cut and paste. WHAT A MESS!" He speaks loudly and does not seem to be bothered that others might hear.
>
> Prosecutor Göran, 35+, first instance court,
> fieldnotes hearing/break, fraud, Sweden

Initially, Prosecutor Göran seems to consciously work on his temper – pacing quickly in a circle, but long-winded and courteous when asking the police officer about the case, and making sure to get all the information right. When he hears that the fault in the photo numbering is due to the police officer having cut and paste the identification numbers from a previous investigation, he breaks out into moral rage, kicking the wall as a physical outlet for his anger, but maintaining control over his voice throughout the phone call, so as to avoid the police officer at the other end of the line noticing his outburst. This somewhat mismatched combination of a backstage raging body and a dispassionate frontstage voice ends with a cold reprimand to the police officer ("Don't do this again"), as a subtle but paternalistic indication of blame. For a short while after the phone call, Prosecutor Göran seems to be completely immersed in his anger, body and voice aligned, and not caring about how it makes him look. As a form of venting, his fervent anger spins into a more general frustration with police officers not following their guidelines. He then returns to court with a calm demeanour. When the trial resumes a few minutes later, Göran's intense anger is nowhere to be seen:

> As soon as the court proceeding starts again, Prosecutor Göran requests the floor and states in a neutral voice, "I would like to immediately announce that I intend to make another examination." The judge approves and the court makes a call to the police officer. Prosecutor Göran sounds calm and pedagogical during the short examination: "If I frame the question like this, are there any peculiarities with your PM?" and "Now that you can view your PM in hindsight and also the material from the

photo confrontation again, how sure are you that it is photo number six that shows the defendant?" The police officer says that he is sure.

Prosecutor Göran, 35+, first instance court,
fieldnotes hearing, fraud, Sweden

Back in the courtroom, Prosecutor Göran's anger is low in its intensity and only visible through his thoroughness and correct but somewhat condescending formulations ("If I frame the question like this, are there any peculiarities with your PM?", "Now when you can view your PM in hindsight…"), indicating a drive to save his face in the examination with the police officer. In this way, Prosecutor Göran has both saved the evidence provided by the photo line-up to strengthen the case and re-established his status. The judge's immediate acceptance of this new and unexpected examination shows her awareness of the break in the interaction order and a willingness to get the proceedings back on track.

As this (and the earlier sequence involving Judge Giorgio) demonstrates, anger, when linked to surprise, should not be released frontstage, since it poses a threat to professional conduct. The focus frontstage is to stall the situation, while avoiding the risk of turning the surprise into professional shame by being accused of malpractice. One could speculate that this high demand to solve the problem while displaying control to some extent functions to block anger. Once backstage, both Judge Giorgio and Prosecutor Göran explode into brief but intense anger, but Prosecutor Göran, who in contrast to Judge Giorgio, is not among colleagues, performs a split between his angry body and his calm voice in his efforts to obtain the information he needs to save face and re-establish a composed demeanour. When comparing both these episodes of exploding anger, their performative side comes to the fore. Judge Giorgio uses strong language ("FUCK", "SHIT") and Prosecutor Göran pointedly kicks the wall hard, both using displays that seem to require an audience, which is perhaps also a partial reason why the outbursts were so brief.[2] When returning to court, anger instead lingers in the form of the low-intensity energy needed to sort out the muddled situation. As described here, anger is first postponed, then performed in a brief and intense way, and finally simmers and energises, all the time being aligned with the immediate task of solving the unexcepted problem.

Easy come, easy go – swift frustration

People feel frustrated when they feel "a perceived discrepancy between their beliefs and goals" (Miceli and Castelfranchi, 2019: 14). As we saw in the earlier chapter on nagging narratives, legal professionals get frustrated when

2 Stina, who shadowed prosecutor Göran, noted the strong reaction as somewhat out of place, as if he augmented the gesture for her to see, which resulted in it coming across as a little too aggressive.

lay people or other legal professionals do not deliver the clean and well-demarcated narratives that they depend on to prove their case (prosecutors) or make robust evaluations (judges). *Frustration* is therefore a common interactional response to contradictory or reluctant accounts during examinations and other presentations in court. In the next extract, which is taken from a murder trial in the first instance in Italy, Prosecutor Anna (30+) gets frustrated by a witness, whose brother is accused of murdering their father, when he shows reluctance to answer questions about issues that he has disclosed during the preliminary investigation. When we enter the examination, the witness has just mentioned that a close friend of the defendant told him that a potential motive for the murder might be that the father had interfered in his brother's romantic relationship. Prosecutor Anna's frustration comes out in the form of persistent questioning interspersed with shouting.[3]

PROSECUTOR ANNA: Excuse me, but you talked about this affair that involved your father and your brother's girlfriend. I guess you have some knowledge of the kind of relationship we are talking about. Let's try to contextualize.

WITNESS: I didn't know.

PROSECUTOR ANNA: But then you got to know about it? [annoyed tone of voice]

WITNESS: Yes.

PROSECUTOR ANNA: So, what kind of relationship was it?

WITNESS: I don't know. It didn't last long. I didn't have the chance to see them together.

PROSECUTOR ANNA: Yes, but they did see each other, how frequently? [disappointed] GIVE US SOME MORE INDICATIONS!

WITNESS: I don't know. I knew that from this guy...

PROSECUTOR ANNA: Who raised the issue?

WITNESS: I did.

PROSECUTOR ANNA: The guy said that it was [the defendant's] girlfriend? How was this relationship described?

3 To find someone guilty of murder, the prosecutor needs to prove a murderous intent, that the defendant intended to kill or was indifferent to this outcome, but does not need to prove a motive for the killing. From this perspective Prosecutor Anna's insistence on following this line of questioning is not entirely rational. When she read the police report she had an idea that the father's interference in his son's romantic affair might be a possible motive, and she decided to try to find out more to test her idea.

WITNESS: I don't know.

PROSECUTOR ANNA: But there was an interest from your brother?

WITNESS: I think so.

PROSECUTOR ANNA: And did the girl reciprocate?

WITNESS: I don't know.

Prosecutor Anna, 30+, first instance court,
fieldnotes hearing, murder, Italy

In this extract, Prosecutor Anna has tried to draw information out of the reluctant witness for some time, and her anger reflects the halting interaction. The examination does not flow and she does not get the answers she is expecting or hoping for. Anger here is linked to a temporal experience of being stuck, coupled with the knowledge that showing anger will increase the risk of becoming more stuck and getting no answers at all, and that anger thus needs to be controlled. At the beginning of the exert, Prosecutor Anna's temper is already somewhat taut, and she insinuates that the witness knows more than he is saying ("Excuse me", "I guess you have some knowledge…", "try to contextualize"), indicating that she can see through his evasive answers. As the witness continues to give short answers and Prosecutor Anna keeps pushing for more details and a coherent narrative, her frustration grows ("GIVE US SOME MORE INDICATIONS!"). Her shouting does not influence the witness's answers, and she goes back to her normal voice, but she poses her sometimes suggestive questions ("But there was an interest from your brother?") in a rapid tempo, posing a new question directly after the previous one and leaving little time for the witness to actually answer.

In Sweden and Italy, prosecutors are expected to ask more open questions, and posing this type of narrow, suggestive questions usually implies that they are looking for a specific answer, such as a particular form of wording that the witness used during the police interrogation, or that they want to use the uncooperative witness to drive their own narrative of the event. In the first scenario, their frustration increases when they do not get the answers they want. In the second, the lack of answers does not matter, but it may still constitute a risky strategy because the judge or the defence lawyer can complain that they are posing leading questions. As we see in the next extract, Prosecutor Anna tries to actually get some answers out of the witness, and her frustration builds as a result of her lack of success. When we now return to the scene, prosecutor Anna is showing her anger openly. At this point, the judge, and then the defence lawyer, intervenes:

PROSECUTOR ANNA [angry]: WHY DID THE FRIEND THINK THAT THIS COULD BE THE MOTIVE? It seems a bit weird that [name of the friend] mentioned this girl without knowing anything else.

WITNESS: Maybe he said that [my brother] couldn't make it, he wanted something more.

JUDGE: Wait, prosecutor, the witness isn't clear. Did [name of the friend] say that the defendant was not able to stay with the girl?

Witness stutters.

JUDGE: So, [name of the friend] said that the defendant confided in him that he had some difficulties in staying with girls?

WITNESS: Yes.

JUDGE: But what kind of difficulties? He wasn't able to have a relationship, or were they physical difficulties?

WITNESS: Emotional ones.

PROSECUTOR ANNA: You referred before to a possible discussion between your father and the girl. Can you explain what you mean by that?

WITNESS: I don't know.

PROSECUTOR ANNA: But you cannot say that they had a discussion and then that you don't know.

DEFENCE LAWYER [interrupts]: He said, "a conversation".

PROSECUTOR ANNA [angry tone towards the defence lawyer]: I do not mean in an angry tone.

PROSECUTOR ANNA: CAN YOU REPORT IN A COMPLETE WAY, INSTEAD OF LITTLE BY LITTLE, WHAT [NAME OF THE FRIEND] SAID?

Witness starts answering in an angry tone.

PROSECUTOR ANNA [In a calm tone]: But you did not ask for further explanations about this, the terms, the causes, the motives for your father going to this girl to talk with her?

WITNESS: No.

Prosecutor Anna, 30+, first instance court,
fieldnotes hearing, murder, Italy

It is clear that the witness does not want to talk about what the defendant's friend might have said about a possible motive. As a last resort, to make the witness comply, Prosecutor Anna starts shouting ("WHY DID THE FRIEND THINK THAT THIS COULD BE THE MOTIVE?"). At this point, the witness develops his answer into a full sentence for the first time ("Maybe he said that [my brother] couldn't make it, he wanted something more."), and this is when the judge intervenes. The witness's use of the word 'maybe' can be interpreted as defiance towards the court, and the judge does not comment on Prosecutor Anna's angry shouting, but on the witness's lack of clarity.[4] The judge poses a couple of follow-up questions that unsettle the witness (stutters) and provide time for Prosecutor Anna to calm down. When she takes over again, she has lowered her voice and continues in her efforts to draw out answers from the witness. When the defence lawyer intervenes she explodes again, first telling the defence lawyer off by saying that he is nit-picking (a discussion need not imply conflict), and then turning to the witness ("CAN YOU REPORT IN A COMPLETE WAY, INSTEAD OF LITTLE BY LITTLE, WHAT [NAME OF THE FRIEND] SAID?"). Now, the witness gets angry and Prosecutor Anna immediately backs down, continuing her questions in a markedly calm tone. Even though prosecutors have a high positional status in court, since they direct the presentation of the case and hold examinations, their situational status during an examination can vary depending on their interactional success or failure (cf. Kemper, 1978). A witness, who is often someone with low positional status, may cause the prosecutor to lose their footing in the court situation by preventing them from obtaining the evidence they need. From this perspective, Prosecutor Anna's explosive anger demonstrates a situational failure and loss of status. When the witness is first confronted by the judge, and then gets angry himself, Anna regains her sense of control in the situation and her anger quickly fades.

As we can see from both extracts, Prosecutor Anna moves in and out of brief expressions of angry frustration. Constant anger is not productive as a means of obtaining information, since it risks evoking a breakdown in the trust of the witness and indignation from the other legal professionals. Both the defence lawyer and the judge may accuse her of posing leading questions, and most importantly the judge might turn against her case (cf. Bitsch, 2019). Instead, Prosecutor Anna's anger simmers as an underlying drive to keep on pursuing her line of questioning, and moves in and out of expressive anger to prove a point or try to move the questioning forward. During the whole examination she looks straight at the witness and does not display any evident outward signs, such as blushing or shaking, to indicate shame at losing her temper or breaking with the norms of court conduct.[5] This presumably stems from the fact that she is convinced that the witness is lying, or not telling the whole truth, but it also illustrates the cultural acceptance of anger displays found in Italy (Konewko, 2016). Linking back to the different aspects of anger, Prosecutor Anna's frustration continuously stems from the witness's unwillingness to answer, but whereas her anger is focused on obtaining information during the first part of her examination, when this fails the focus

4 There is a specific word for this in Italian, 'omertà', meaning the use of vague language to protect someone by avoiding telling the whole truth.

5 When legal professionals whom we shadowed lost their temper and felt ashamed about it, they often made excuses or tried to justify their temperamentality to the researcher after the episode. In this situation, Prosecutor Anna did neither, indicating a lack of remorse or shame at breaking with emotion rules (compare Judge Britta on page 45).

of her anger seems to shift towards making the witness himself look bad in order to discredit his reliability.

Swift anger is not only used by prosecutors and defence lawyers during examinations, but also by judges when presiding over trials. In the next extract, Judge Marcello (50+, Italy) displays strategic anger when he harshly rebukes two lay persons in the public gallery during the defence lawyer's closing statement during a rape trial, and then immediately turns back to the defence lawyer to speak calmly:

> There is noise in the courtroom, people are talking. Judge Marcello first rebukes some lawyers, then takes the microphone and, raising the tone of his voice, turns to some people in the public gallery: "Excuse me, who are you? You, over there, please stand up." The man does not answer, but turns away to leave, and Judge Marcello says, "No, no, first tell me who you are." The man replies that he is the father of one of the defendants". Judge Marcello immediately shouts: "GET OUT OF THE COURTROOM IMMEDIATELY. IMMEDIATELY OUT!" He turns to another person in the public gallery: "The lady at the back... you... [points at her with his finger] you have to keep the [COVID] mask on if you want to remain in the courtroom." He then turns his attention back to the defence lawyer: "I apologize, attorney. The fact..."
>
> Judge Marcello, 50+, first instance court,
> fieldnotes hearing, rape, Italy

In this situation, anger initiates immediate action. When Judge Marcello gets angry, he intervenes straight away, instead of pondering about the right solution in the way described earlier in the surprise episodes involving Judge Giorgio and Prosecutor Göran. In this situation, Judge Marcello needed to act immediately to address the disorder in the courtroom, and having the ability to act quickly and resolutely can trump any potential legal incorrectness. Both Judge Marcello and Prosecutor Anna were in the midst of a performance and were unable take a break before deciding on how to move forward in a legally correct and emotionally effective way. Judge Marcello's quick return to a calm and polite demeanour ("The lady at the back...", "I apologize, attorney"), shows that spontaneity need not signify a loss of control. Anger can "bleed over into unrelated contexts" (Maroney, 2012: 1265), but as demonstrated by both Prosecutor Anna and Judge Marcello, when used as a tool focused on specific goals, it does not have to do so. This does not mean that anger is good or bad in a normative sense in these situations, it just means that anger is employed to achieve rational goals.

Time after time – confidence and persistent anger

If some anger is swift and comes and goes easily, anger can also be persistent. While we link the feeling of surprise to problem-solving anger in the short term, anger that persists can affect feelings of confidence in the task at hand

and mis/trust towards individuals or the group that an individual represents. To illustrate a common source of this type of long-acting anger, we will turn to Judge Konrad (55+, Sweden), who was handling a large fraud case in which his irritation at the prosecutor's formulation of the indictment and charges persisted throughout the entirety of the court proceedings, which lasted several weeks:

First trial day, backstage

During one of the pauses, Judge Konrad expresses irritation at how the prosecutor has formulated the indictment and engages in a commentary about the indictment, highlighting different legal problems with its current formulation and referring to earlier rulings that have employed a different construction. Partly turning to the lay judges, partly speaking to himself, he says that he hopes to get the prosecutor to change the indictment. "I've been at him. So that he understands that I'm suspicious."

Second trial day, backstage

Before the trial starts the following day, Judge Konrad tells the lay judges that he needed to "sleep on it", and will now address the prosecutor directly during the trial.

Second trial day, frontstage

Looking at the prosecutor and with a slightly raised, earnest voice he says, "My thought is that we will go over the formulation of the charges once again." He then starts talking about the two criminal code paragraphs that define the fraud offence, asking, "And now I wonder why, is there anything I do not understand? Is there a mixture of the first and the second paragraph?" Referring to one of the incidents that had been dealt with on the previous day, he continues, asking, "Why should it be perceived as a case of aggravated fraud? I want to make sure that this is sorted out so that there is no more [confusion on this issue]. Is it the first or second paragraph that applies? Or is it some kind of mixture, and why is that mixture needed." Judge Konrad speaks quickly and finishes his commentary looking sternly at the prosecutor, asking, "Have I made myself clear?" The prosecutor answers "Very clear. Great." And to demonstrate that he is taking the judge's comments seriously, he makes a concerned gesture, putting his hand over his mouth and looking down at his papers.

Judge Konrad, 50+, first instance court, fraud, Sweden

Taken together, the first two days of the trial can illustrate the temporal evolution of anger. At first Konrad airs and tests his irritation backstage to the lay judges and the court clerk. Before acting on it, he seems to be looking to have his anger validated, both in a legal sense, on the basis of previous court judgements, and collegially. The frustration over the charges grows in intensity as Judge Konrad becomes more confident in his own perception of how the case should be legally assessed. His irritation is charged up to engage in what is an uncommonly active way of directing the prosecutor during court proceedings ("My thought is that we will go over the formulation of the charges once again."). In the Swedish legal context, judges, it is thought, should not intervene to amend or clarify the indictment, and therefore they rarely explicitly say that they find the charges problematic but instead try to hint to the prosecutor, as Judge Konrad had done on the first day ("He understands that I'm suspicious.") (cf. Bergman Blix and Wettergren, 2019). The prosecutor does not seem to get the hint and, during this two-week long trial, Judge Konrad returns to the formulation of the charges, asking for the prosecutor's view on the severity of specific incidents, the overall 'modus operandi' (technique) that the prosecutor claims the defendant is using, and how the two legal paragraphs that define the fraud offence should be interpreted. After one of these 'hints', the prosecutor says that he wants to change the statement of the criminal act as charged and starts expounding on the new charge. Judge Konrad quickly realises that this is not in line with the changes he wants and dismisses the changes of the indictment suggested by the prosecutor, stating that they involve ambiguities and that it is better to keep the statement of the criminal act as it is. In a neutral but very brief reply, the prosecutor says, "Then I do not wish to change. We keep it. Absolutely", signalling compliance and cooperativeness.

The Swedish legal practice of linking the impartiality principle to the judge refraining from uttering anything that might hurt the defence builds irritation into the process. Judges get frustrated when prosecutors do not understand their hints, and prosecutors get frustrated and worried when they do not understand what judges are trying to convey to them. Both are eager to send and receive their respective messages, but are set up to fail due to an inability to be direct. In a subsequent interview with the prosecutor in Judge Konrad's trial, he described the judge as "very nice, but he was angry with the defence lawyer" (Prosecutor Patrik, 45+, Sweden), which suggests that the hostile interaction does not occupy the prosecutor's understanding of the trial in retrospect. Still, it is clear that Judge Konrad's irritation and hints failed to communicate what the judge had intended. Our Swedish data contain several examples of judges thinking they are being crystal clear in their hints, while the prosecutors involved completely fail to understand what they mean. In contrast, as we saw in the appellate court trial in the United States (page 34), Judge Frederick explicitly stated what he thought was wrong with the way the case had been put together. Refraining from speaking one's mind about the way a case has been formulated is thus not a universal interpretation of what impartiality implies in practice.[6] Judge Konrad's anger makes him

6 This might be changing in Swedish courts as well. In a recent case involving rape of a minor, the appellate court found that the charge should have been sexual assault and not rape, and

vulnerable since he needs to balance demands for impartiality, interpreted as refraining from intervention, with a need to intervene in order to be able to make a legally correct ruling. Judge Frederick's anger was direct and left his confidence about making a ruling intact.

Returning to the fraud case, Judge Konrad confided to the clerk and the lay judges during a break that the prosecutor's thoughts on changing the indictment made him nervous:

> **Third trial day, backstage**
>
> Judge Konrad says that if they had gone along with these changes they would only have been able to sentence the defendant for fraud and not aggravated fraud. "That's why I backed down and the prosecutor understood that it was for his sake." Turning to the clerk, judge Konrad says that he "got some stomach ache" listening to the changes suggested by the prosecutor, and that he felt a "pressing worry" about how he should deal with it. He continues saying that he decided to "put it on the table" and that he reasoned with himself, "Should I be here with a stomach ache?" Judge Konrad then starts to talk about ways judges can be mean to prosecutors in the written court judgement.
>
> Judge Konrad, 50+, first instance court, fraud, Sweden

As we can see from this episode, Judge Konrad's irritation intersects with feeling nervous and worried, which shifts the direction of his anger slightly. Initially his irritation centred on the formulation of the indictment itself, but the proposed changes to the charges instead actualised irritation from him being dependent on the legal frames that the prosecutor provided. Since Judge Konrad feels that the suggested changes would limit his space for agency, his irritation taps into frustration. Interestingly, this shift in the direction of his irritation seems to affect Judge Konrad in a more physical way, as he starts to speak about "stomach ache" and "a pressing worry", hinting at a greater intensity than in earlier interactions on this subject. In other words, his frustration seems to move to a more foregrounded position, but is still not openly articulated as anger.

While still annoyed with the prosecutor, these emotions are diffused by imagining ways of getting back at the prosecutor later, by writing a judging that is mean to the prosecutor. While Judge Konrad's forward-looking anger in reality led only to hinting and failed communication with the prosecutor, his forward-looking fantasy about revenge, by subjecting the prosecutor to status degradation in the written ruling, seems to relieve some pressure so

acquitted the defendant without trying the alternative charge, since the prosecutor had not included it in the indictment. The Supreme Court stated that the court should not refrain from trying an alternative legal charge if it finds that the evidence presented covers an alternative charge that has not been included in an indictment (NJA 2021 p. 827).

that he is able to move on in the moment. As the trial continues with no adjustments by the prosecution, Judge Konrad's irritation surfaces less often, as he seems to have found a way to deal with the formulation of the indictment that works for him and that does not limit his choices in relation to the verdict. During an interview a couple of weeks after the court proceedings had ended, the judge's anger has settled into a clearer and uncomplicated version of itself:

After trial, interview

On that matter, I was irritated with the prosecutor from the start and eh very... determined. And that only... Writing the verdict only made me more convinced, so that was not a problem.

Judge Konrad, 50+, first instance court, fraud, Sweden

In this retrospective reflection, Judge Konrad links his irritation during the court proceedings with certainty and determination, eliminating those moments when his anger also gave rise to insecurity and worry. When the grounds for irritation no longer threaten agency and choice, irritation can become empowering and be related to confidence and comfort. This difference between the at-times chaotic and uncertain unfolding of emotions while working with a case, and the more controlled and clean depiction of emotions in later interviews is common in our material. Once the uncertainty and the decision have been settled, emotions are put in order (Bergman Blix and Törnqvist, 2024). In line with the other examples in this chapter, it is not primarily the feeling itself that is managed, but rather the situational orientation that shapes the way anger evolves.

On a final note, these occasions of persistent anger can, in the longer run, turn into a kind of *stale resentment*, a hostile emotionality that relates to a generalised mistrust against other legal professionals or a frustration with organisational/institutional structures, thus feeding on the links between anger and ideas of fairness and honesty (Miceli and Castelfranchi, 2019). Stale resentment tends to be directed towards groups that the legal professionals depend on to do their work. As we saw with Prosecutor Göran in this chapter and Prosecutor Tess in the last chapter (p. 27), police officers constitute a group that can elicit this type of resentment,[7] but defence lawyers are also common targets, while judges can hold long-term grudges against individual counsel and prosecutors, who make their work difficult, as indicated by remarks such as "that's one of those people you need to keep an eye on" (Judge

7 Since trust is key in making legal work possible, this kind of resentment is often reserved for a more limited part of the other profession, narrowed down by specific epithets, for example young and "reckless cowboy"-police officers or reluctant, "old fossil" investigators (Törnqvist, 2017).

Ellinor, 30+, Sweden) about a victim counsel whom a judge reported for malpractice.

The staleness of this emotion is linked to its longevity, which involves a settled perspective. This resentment is prompted when a legal professional acts in an expected, negative way; for example a defence lawyer 'padding the bill', a lame and unengaged victim counsel, or a lay judge falling asleep during a hearing. While resentment may be elicited by different types of incidents, it is present even when it is not felt in the moment. In our data, stale resentment is mostly backgrounded, but it can easily trigger momentary anger. This is evident in our interview data, where legal professionals could start talking about a particular incident in a calm and unengaged manner, but moved into anger the more they became immersed in the situation they were recounting.

References

Barbalet Jack. (2009) Consciousness, Emotions, and Science. In: D Hopkins, J Kleres, H Flam, H. Kuzmics (eds) *Theorizing Emotions*. Frankfurt: Campus.

Barbalet Jack. (2011) Emotions beyond regulation: Backgrounded emotions in science and trust. *Emotion Review* 3: 36–43.

Bergman Blix Stina. (2015) Professional emotion management as a rehearsal process. *Professions and Professionalism* 5: 1–15.

Bergman Blix Stina. (2022) Making independent decisions together: Rational emotions in legal adjudication. *Symbolic Interaction* 45: 50–71.

Bergman Blix Stina and Törnqvist Nina. (2024) Navigating uncertainty and negotiating trust in judicial deliberations. *Frontier in Sociology* 9: 1–11

Bergman Blix Stina and Wettergren Åsa. (2016) A sociological perspective on emotions in the judiciary. *Emotion Review* 8: 32–37.

Bergman Blix Stina and Wettergren Åsa. (2018) *Professional Emotions in Court: A Sociological Perspective*. London: Routledge.

Bergman Blix Stina and Wettergren Åsa. (2019) The emotional interaction of judicial objectivity. *Oñati Socio-Legal Series* 9: 726–746.

Bitsch Anne. (2019) Voldtektens geografi. En studie av den rettslige forvaltningen av seksuelt medborgerskap i Norge. PhD thesis. Department of Sociology and Human Geography, University of Oslo, Oslo.

Bogosavljevic Katarina and Kilty Jennifer M. (2021) 'Now, the question here is who to believe': Criminalising HIV nondisclosure, emotions and determinations of credibility in R. v. TS. *Emotions and Society* 3: 209–225.

Flower Lisa. (2018) Doing loyalty: Defense lawyers' subtle dramas in the courtroom. *Journal of Contemporary Ethnography* 47: 226–254.

Flower Lisa. (2020) *Interactional Justice: The Role of Emotions in the Performance of Loyalty*. Abingdon, Oxon: Routledge.

Goffman Erving. (1956) Embarrassment and social organization. *The American Journal of Sociology* 62: 264–271.

Goffman Erving. (1959) *The Presentation of Self in Everyday Life*. New York: Doubleday.

Goffman Erving. (1972) *Relations in Public: Microstudies of the Public Order*. New York: Harper & Row.

Hochschild Arlie Russell. (1983) *The Managed Heart: Commercialization of Human Feeling*. Los Angeles: University of California Press.

Holmes Mary. (2004) The Importance of being angry: Anger in political life. *European Journal of Social Theory* 7: 123–132.

Kemper Theodore D. (1978) *A Social Interaction Theory of Emotions*. New York: John Wiley & Sons.
Konewko Simonetta Milli. (2016) *Neorealism and the "New" Italy: Compassion in the Development of Italian Identity*. New York: Palgrave MacMillan.
Kövecses Zoltán. (2009) Cross-cultural experience of anger: A psycholinguistic analysis. In: M Potegal, GS Stemmler and C Spielberger (eds) *International Handbook of Anger: Constituent and Concomitant Biological, Psychological, and Social Processes*. New York: Springer, 157–174.
Landweer Hilge. (2020) Aggressive emotions: from irritation to hatred, contempt and indignation. In: T Szanto and H Landweer (eds) *The Routledge Handbook of Phenomenology of Emotion*. London: Routledge, 441–454.
Maroney Terry A. (2012) Angry judges. *Vanderbilt Law Review* 65: 1207–1286.
Miceli Maria and Castelfranchi Cristiano. (2019) Anger and its cousins. *Emotion Review* 11: 13–26.
Pierce Jennifer L. (2003) "Racing for Innocence": Whiteness, corporate culture, and the backlash against affirmative action. *Qualitative Sociology* 26: 53–70.
Roach Anleu Sharyn and Mack Kathy. (2021) *Judging and Emotion: A Socio-Legal Analysis*. Abingdon, Oxon: Routledge.
Scarduzio Jennifer A. (2011) Maintaining order through deviance? The emotional deviance, power, and professional work of municipal court judges. *Management Communication Quarterly* 25: 283–310.
Scott Susie. (2021) Surprise: A micro-sociological analysis. *Emotions and Society* 3: 191–207.
Shields Stephanie A. (2002) *Speaking from the Heart: Gender and the Social Meaning of Emotion*. Cambridge: Cambridge University Press.
Stollznow Karen. (2024) *Bitch: The Journey of a Word*. Cambridge: Cambridge University Press.
Traister Rebecca. (2023) *Good and Mad: The Revolutionary Power of Women's Anger*. New York: Simon and Schuster.
Törnqvist Nina. (2017) Att göra rätt. En studie om professionell respektabilitet, emotioner och narrativa linjer bland relationsvåldsspecialiserade åklagare (Doing just right: A study on professional respectability, emotions and narrative lines among prosecutors specialised in relationship violence). PhD thesis. Department of Criminolog, Stockholm University, Stockholm.
Törnqvist Nina and Wettergren Åsa. (2023) Epistemic emotions in prosecutorial decision-making. *Journal of Law and Society* 50: 208–230.
van Oorschot Irene. (2021) *The Law Multiple: Judgment and Knowledge in Practice*. Cambridge: Cambridge University Press.
Wettergren Åsa and Bergman Blix Stina. (2021) Comparing Culturally Embedded Frames of Judicial Dispassion. In: S Bandes, JL Madeira, K Temple and E Kidd White. (eds) *Research Handbook on Law and Emotion*. Northampton, MA: Edward Elgar Publishing, 146–163.
Wingfield Adia Harvey. (2010) Are some emotions marked "whites only"? racialized feeling rules in professional workplaces. *Social Problems* 57: 251–268.
Wingfield Adia Harvey. (2021) The (un) managed heart: Racial contours of emotion work in gendered occupations. *Annual Review of Sociology* 47: 197–212.
Zerubavel Eviatar. (1985) *Hidden Rhythms: Schedules and Calendars in Social Life*. Berkeley: University of California Press.

4 Respectable rage

The law represents the codification of morality, guarding the boundaries of what is considered right and wrong. Society has decided that certain acts, such as murder, theft, and rape, are wrong, and if a person is found guilty of committing such acts, society shows its disapproval by imposing predetermined penalties.[1] As depicted in the introduction, legal scholars and philosophers have argued that moral condemnation in the form of anger or outrage should be expected or even required in criminal courts (Solomon, 1995), and that it can be seen as a righteous symbol of justice (Maroney, 2012: 1215):

> The righteously angry judge is angry for good reasons, experiences and expresses that anger in a well-regulated manner, and uses her anger to motivate and carry out the tasks within her authority. Righteously angry judges deserve not our condemnation but our approval.

Maroney's depiction of righteous anger includes the condemnation of both *the offences* that are dealt with in court and breaches of *respectful behaviour* during court proceedings. While the former involves a focus on the defendant's potential guilt, the latter includes all actors, lay persons, and legal professionals who are involved in the legal process. The ideal that the judge, as a guardian of society's moral boundaries, needs to have a capacity for outrage must be balanced against the judge's role as the guardian of a just process. As we showed in Chapter 2, this latter ideal of ensuring a just process supersedes by far the ideal of the morally condemnatory judge (or legal professional in general). In legal terms, the judge's professional role is not so much centred on condemning the offence as such, but rather on ensuring a just process that adheres to the principles of objectivity, impartiality, and independence. In practical terms, legal professionals' main source of anger is related to getting the stories told in court suitable for legal evaluations and assessments.

1 The word 'boundaries' is important here; not everything that is deemed morally wrong is illegal, but the law specifies the ultimate boundaries of what society considers to be accepted moral behaviour.

DOI: 10.4324/9781003330592-4

Still, moral condemnation lies at the heart of the law and in this chapter, we return to the *what*-question of Chapter 2 to explore anger as a balancing act between different ideals: the ideal of a just process and the ideal of moral condemnation – the art of performing respectable rage. To distinguish between these two ideals, we use 'moral outrage' to signify the moral condemnation of offences, and 'legal pathos' (cf. Minissale, 2023) to signify anger as a result of moral loyalty to a just process. By analysing instances of moral outrage and legal pathos, we show how these ideals are sometimes conflicting, sometimes intertwined, and are given different weight depending on legal tradition and emotional regime. Moral outrage can take different directions aiming towards retribution, recognition, or resignation.

Moral speech to defendants

Open expressions of moral outrage directed at defendants generally appear at the end of a hearing in the form of a *moral speech*, when judges deliver their decision. Moral outrage brings to mind strong emotions, but can just as well be delivered in a mechanical way that is seemingly devoid of upset emotions, but that still clearly communicates moral condemnation. We find that moral outrage is directed at defendants in all the countries examined, but with clear between-country differences. In the United States and Scotland, moral evaluation and condemnation are entangled with legal reasoning, while in Sweden and Italy they are separated. In the extract below, Judge Imogen (45+, Trial court judge, USA), gives a moral speech to a defendant when delivering a probation decision:

> Judge Imogen reads the presentencing report and then turns to the defence lawyer: [sceptical tone] "One of the things the description of the facts outlined is that the weapon was found *warm*, with an empty magazine not in the gun but next to the seat and the testimony on who fired the shots was evasive. I don't understand *why* is that? [sombre tone] And *no part* of taking responsibility, it is concerning to me. I was unimpressed with that testimony." She turns from the defence lawyer to the defendant [stern tone] "You've got nothing else to lose at this point except *your freedom.*"
>
> Judge Imogen, 45+, first instance court, probation, USA

When judges explain the reasoning behind their decisions, this links to ideals of procedural justice (Tyler and Bies, 1990). The ruling in court should not only be a matter for legal professionals, the defendant should also understand the reasoning behind the verdict. Judge Imogen's reproach fits well with Maroney's (2012: 1215) depiction of righteous anger in that she expresses her condemnation in a calm and controlled manner, and expresses concern about the defendants' behaviour. On the other hand, she does not look at the defendant during her reasoning, but at the defence lawyer, only directing her final crescendo (stern voice) at the defendant ("You've got nothing else to lose at this point except *your freedom*"). Judge Imogen's speech constitutes a typical example of the moral outrage found in our data from the United States and Scotland, in that she integrates factual and moral reasoning. When judges make probation decisions, they evaluate the evidence in the case. At the start of Judge Imogen's speech, she counts the strength of the evidence by putting them on a timeline (warm weapon, magazine on the seat, evasive testimony), and then adds her moral evaluation of the defendant's testimony (not taking responsibility). In this way, her decision comes across as being motivated both by the facts of the case and the defendant's behaviour during the hearing. Her reference to not having taken responsibility during the hearing implicitly links to her moral outrage at the offence. Taking responsibility for the offence after the event or in court, in legal terms showing remorse, can serve as a mitigating factor in sentencing in US (and Scottish) courts. The task of evaluating remorse in this way introduces moral evaluations into the judge's reasoning (cf. Field and Tata, 2023).

There are also instances in which moral outrage is not linked to evaluating remorse, but is rather linked directly to the act, as when Judge Fiona (70+, high court, Scotland), having recounted the events in a case, remarks "I see no decency in what you did", or when a judge focuses attention on the defendant's appearance, as in the case of a defendant showing up visibly high on drugs, or in other ways not showing respect towards the court. Here, moral outrage does not seem to fill any purpose in relation to the legal evaluation. In the case below, as his client had entered the courtroom, the defence lawyer had warned Judge Ian (50+, Sheriffs court, Scotland) that his client was "not firing on all cylinders today". The judge did not look at the defendant at first, but down at his papers in order to read about the case. He then lifted his gaze when he realised that the defendant was supposed to be participating in a drug rehabilitation program:

> Judge Ian looks between the defence lawyer and his papers, he speaks in a very clear voice: "[Defendants name]'s participation in the program is crucial. [turning to the defendant] You can graduate, and if you don't, *you become the looser.*" Defence lawyer says that the defendant looks terrible; Judge Ian leans back and agrees with him. He leans forward again and sighs, "he's close to death, wouldn't take much. Let me speak to him." The defence lawyer nods and Judge Ian speaks straight to the defendant: [serious tone] "Have you looked at yourself in the mirror today…?" Before the defendant has a chance to answer Judge Ian says [sarcastic tone] "You look like death warmed up!" His expression has hardened a little bit across his face, the corners of his mouth are somewhat turned down and his forehead slightly wrinkled.
>
> Judge Ian, 50+, first instance court, drug sales, Scotland

In this extract, moral outrage is evident both in the words used and in the judge's gazes and nonverbal expressions. Judge Ian looks at the defence lawyer when stressing the importance of the rehabilitation program ("[it] is crucial") and then straight at the defendant when adding a rebuke ("...if you don't, you become the loser"). The defence lawyer and judge then start talking about the defendant in the third person ("he looks terrible", "close to death"), with the judge sighing, while his voice and face become stern when directing a final admonition straight at the defendant ("looked yourself in the mirror", "death warmed up").

It can be noted that integrating moral outrage into the legal judgement seems to open up for emotions that are more or less effective in the situation. If Judge Imogen's moral outrage was dressed up as concern, Judge Ian's outrage verges on contempt, both at the defendant's failure to participate in drug treatment and at his appearance. Previous research has shown that when people feel contempt, they focus less on the wrongdoing as such and more on the (bad) person that they deem unable to change (Tausch et al., 2011). In Maroney's terms (2012), moral anger turning into contempt loses its caring function focused on reintegration into society, but it also loses in rationality, as it serves no clear function in the legal process.

We have no examples from Sweden or Italy of judges integrating legal and moral evaluations in the moral speeches they direct at defendants. In these civil law countries, judges rarely direct moral speeches at adult defendants, but they are considered part of the institutionalised to-do list in youth trials, after the sentence has been delivered.[2] In the extract below, Judge Robert (60+, Sweden), directs a moral speech to an adult defendant, motivated by the fact that this was the defendant's 'last chance' to stay out of prison since he had already been given a conditional sentence on two previous occasions:

> When everyone starts to get up to leave the courtroom, Judge Robert interrupts: "Well, I'll preach a little too." He looks at the defendant and begins with a tired and mechanical tone: "You have been lucky; you have received two conditional sentences. If I'm sitting in court and see you again and it's a prison-level crime [he does not take a break to allow the interpreter to keep up, and he has now gotten into his speech and preaches in a low, stern voice]. The district court will not turn a blind eye the next time, do you understand? [raises voice] Stay away from here!"
>
> Judge Robert, 60+, first instance court, fieldnotes hearing, theft, Sweden

2 In 2002, the Swedish National Council for Crime Prevention published a report (Frodlund, 2002) showing that young offenders understood very little of what was happening at their own trials, generating a debate among legal professionals about how to manage young offenders. Today, moral speeches once judges have delivered their judgments is standard practice in youth trials.

The fact that people had already started to stand up ready to leave, and that Judge Robert gave a little introduction to his speech ("Well, I'll preach a little too") illustrates the clear division between delivering the sentence and acknowledging the offence as a moral offence, and not only a legal one. The speech is not only separated symbolically from the sentencing, but also in its content. Judge Robert's speech does not refer to any aspects of the criminal act per se, as was the case in Judge Imogen's speech, or to the defendant's appearance, as was the case in Judge Ian's rebuke, but restricts its focus to a legal rule – after two conditional sentences, prison is unavoidably the next step. Nevertheless, the 'agreement' associated with a conditional sentence, that is, that the state imposes a lesser sentence on the condition that the offender will not commit more offences, is based on trust. Judge Robert's moral outrage might perhaps be based on the defendant's having broken or exploited trust that had previously been placed in him by the state. Judge Robert's decision to deliver a moral speech in this rather trivial case of theft is also in line with the results of a study on Danish judges (Johansen and Laursen, 2023), which found that judges delivered such moral speeches in less-severe cases that involved lenient sentences, while refraining from moral speeches in severe cases that resulted in indeterminate sentences, arguing that in the latter case the indeterminate sentence spoke for itself. This further emphasises the separation between legal and moral evaluations in that the moral 'add-on' is not considered relevant when the legal evaluation has resulted in a severe sentence.

We would suggest that legal tradition lies behind the differences in the way moral outrage is displayed in the United States and Scotland compared to Sweden and Italy. In the common law systems of the United States and Scotland, moral outrage is integrated into legal reasoning, while in the civil law systems of Sweden and Italy, moral outrage is unusual and is separated from legal reasoning. The civil law systems' basis in written code is aligned with 'formal rationality' (Weber, 1998). When legal professionals follow a correct legal procedure by applying law to facts, the right decision 'emerges'. In this view, legal professionals should always keep their eye on the process rather than on the outcome, and legal proceedings value impersonal and equal treatment (Deflem, 2008), making moral evaluations (morally) suspect. This reasoning is substantiated in one of our earlier studies, in which Swedish judges argued that morality had no bearing on their work (Bergman Blix and Wettergren, 2018: 10, 149), and were often quite perplexed by the fact that we even raised the question. In contrast, common law systems, building on precedent, are often seen as more dynamic in that they are expected to develop and to continuously account for current social circumstances (Dworkin, 1986). In rational terms, this incorporates both formal and substantive logics, making moral evaluations by the judge an integral part of legal decision-making. As indicated in our data, the civil and common law systems' different emphasis and expectations regarding moral loyalty towards the process or the outcome respectively influence the emotional cultures relating which *expressions* of moral outrage focused on defendants are accepted or not accepted. This does not mean that Swedish and Italian judges never *experience* moral outrage towards defendants and their criminal acts (as we will see later in an Italian panel of judges during a fraud case), but one can assume that moral loyalty to the legal process in the form of legal pathos to some extent blocks moral outrage being directed at the criminal act and defendant during the decision-making process.

We can also see that expressions of moral outrage, irrespective of the country in question, are not necessarily felt, but are rather expressed for strategic purposes. In legal cultures that integrate moral speeches into the delivery of sentences, the judge can 'do' moral outrage in the form of lip service. As is evident in all of the cases described above, the judges tended to start their speeches in an emotionally distant 'mechanical tone', which eventually became more emotionally engaged. Playing the part of the morally outraged judge, the judges seemed to shift into angry feelings, expressed with a direct gaze, emphasised words, and stern voices, illustrating that the display of anger can itself generate the experience (Bergman Blix, 2015).[3]

Disappointment at victims and witnesses

While moral outrage at offences is typically directed at defendants, legal professionals' moral anger at victims and witnesses tends to take the form of disappointment when these parties change their stories or fail to appear in court. This feeling of disappointment is based on perceived failures of reciprocity (Lerner et al., 2015), demonstrating the dependence of legal professionals on victims and witnesses telling their stories and participating in hearings for the legal process to function. The dependence of legal professionals on witnesses is obvious in the sense that rulings are in many cases based on oral evidence, but it also reflects the structure of the legal process. The final legal ruling in court emerges from several decisions made along the way, which successively constrain the legal professionals' range of possible actions (Bourdieu, 1986). For example, the prosecutor's decision to prosecute and the judge's decision on coercive measures are partly dependent on their trust in the testimonies given during the preliminary investigation. These preliminary testimonies need to be repeated in court for them to hold up as evidence. When victims or witnesses fail to show up, the evidence can fall apart and the legal professionals' trust in them can be broken (Leiterdorf-Shkedy and Gal, 2019). The legal professionals' anger becomes entangled with shame when previous decisions they have made no longer hold up.

3 As we have stressed earlier, expressions of anger do not necessarily indicate feeling anger, but the changes in embodied displays in these depicted situations (direct gaze, emphasised words, and stern voices) suggest an immersion into an anger experience. This interpretation is further substantiated by the situational cues that make anger a meaningful reaction in these situations.

We have found that the three types of crime on which we have focused (intimate partner violence, fraud, and lethal violence) involve different evaluations of what constitutes morally correct behaviour by victims and witnesses. Moral anger and disappointment are most frequent in cases of intimate partner violence. In the interview extract below, Judge Gabriele (45+, Italy) expresses moral anger and to some extent resentment towards a woman who had retracted her accusations of intimate partner violence. He convicted the husband and asked the prosecutor to charge the woman with perjury:

> At one point, she comes to the hearing and retracts everything, *EVERYTHING*, and I mean everything! [laughs]. Speaking, crying like crazy … because, after all, this woman was clearly in a position to get her husband convicted, … and they had children … or, obviously, falling back into that kind of dynamic, … so she comes, retracts everything. And I remember how the prosecutor, a very capable one, got very angry. … We both got angry, actually, but the prosecutor lost his temper because, clearly, you see a person who is patently telling you things that are not true, okay? Well, practically at the end, I convicted him and sent the record to the prosecutor's office for a perjury case against her. I had to [serious tone]. … You cannot, you see, I mean … from a human perspective, I may even understand that … but … it is not possible then to come to the hearing and read us a movie script! NONSENSE! The prosecutor told her: 'Madam, are you at all aware that we are running a trial here? First you told us one thing, and now you're telling us something else!'
>
> Judge Gabriele, 45+, first instance court,
> post-hearing interview, IPV, Italy

Judge Gabriele articulates his anger at the victim's withdrawal of her story in line with a focus on, and pride in, making an accurate legal judgement, as depicted in our chapter on nagging narratives. Legal professionals cannot do their job if they are not given accurate information. In this case, the evidence was still sufficient for a guilty verdict, but Judge Gabriele expresses moral outrage at the woman feeding the court such obvious lies. When the victim turns the hearing into a 'crying show', using strong emotional expressions, she both undermines respect for the court's proceedings and is treating the legal professionals as if they were stupid. The quote from Gabriele makes it clear that he did not believe that the woman was putting on her show out of malice. He engages in a rudimentary form of empathic attunement, describing that he can understand the woman "falling back into that kind of dynamic", but he clearly separates this "human perspective" from a legal perspective, and initiates a perjury case against her. By lying to their faces, the woman was underestimating or challenging the prosecutor and the judge's status, thus subordinating their task, and by extension the rule of law, to her own personal goals. There is a key sentence at the end of the quote, when

Judge Gabriele becomes outraged ("NONSENSE") highlighting that the victim changed her story ("First you told us one thing, and now you're telling us something else!"). This is important, since it intermingles his personal pride in doing his job with the organisational goals of the legal authority. When the process has come so far, retraction has multiple implications.

In another case of intimate partner violence, Judge Rossella (60+, Italy) explained her anger at a victim who had retracted her story by referring to the victim as "clogg[ing] the machinery of justice with such big dossiers [massive investigations]; the lawyer even asked me for coercive measures against him [the perpetrator], and now [irritated tone] nothing exists anymore". When "the machinery of justice" has already started turning, the victim's retraction moves from being a personal tragedy to an obstruction of justice. And, as indicated by Judge Rossella, the legal professionals' pride in doing a good job and representing justice becomes tarnished by organisational traces left in the machinery – Judge Rossella had ordered coercive measures against a suspect whom she then had to let go, generating feelings of shame for having (in retrospect) made an incorrect legal decision. This also happened to Judge Debora (45+, Italy) in yet another case of intimate partner violence. Debora elaborated on the implications for the suspect and for herself:

> ... I mean, a coercive measure is a measure to be imposed with particular caution, also because it is of a *CUSTODIAL* nature. Being under house arrest is like being *IN JAIL*, and so I had imposed a particularly *STRICT* measure, having, in a sense, [slight sarcastic laughter] trusted the word of this woman. Ehm [sign of hesitation] ...well, a trial in which you initially impose a coercive measure, but that ends with an acquittal, is rather *ABNORMAL*, let's put it that way. Trials are not meant to go in that direction.
>
> Judge Debora, 45+, first instance court, post-hearing interview, IPV, Italy

Judge Debora thus described the implications of the precautionary measures she had ordered using an analogy ("like being *IN JAIL*"), demonstrating an empathic imagination in relation to the suspect, while distancing herself from the alleged victim with sarcastic laughter ("trusted the word of this woman"). Her loss of trust in the woman included a loss of trust in the woman's story and in her reasons for not coming to the trial. She continued: "She may have done this out of fear, but she may also have done this because she got tired of this man or they didn't get along, but anyway... she had no... [sign of hesitation] right to take the children away like that. Without even telling him where she was going." Empathically attuning to someone builds on some level of respect for the person in question, a sense that they are deserving of empathy (Barnett and Mann, 2013), and the woman possibly leaving the country with her children made Judge Debora more prone to empathic attunement with the husband, the suspected abuser. Because she would have to acquit, since the husband was legally speaking not guilty of intimate partner violence, Judge Debora imagined other possible explanations for the woman's actions ("she may also have done this because she got tired of this man or they didn't get along"). In addition, on the basis of this new interpretation of events, the wife was censured and could be accused of breaking the law by abducting the children. Importantly, the timing of the woman's retraction had not "*MADE MY JOB EASIER*. If it is true that when one eh... asks justice for protection and support, one then needs to be at the disposal of justice." (Judge Debora, 45+, Italy)

The anger expressed by these judges all goes back to the fact that the justice process had started in all these cases, and the judges had already invested their professional pride in processing them through the system. When these women retracted their accusations after several legal decisions had already been made, in the form of indictments and coercive measures, they exposed the judges to professional shame, generating anger at those who had made them subject suspects who were subsequently released to restrictive interventions (Scheff, 1990). The judges' anger is both logical and rational when understood from a legal perspective. But it becomes more complicated if there is competition between reality and legality. This has become the case in Sweden, where there has been a shift in perspective over the last decade, with the reluctance of victims to testify in IPV cases having become legitimised and expected by reference to normalisation processes (Törnqvist, 2017). The understanding that women who are subject to violence over time tend to adjust to this violence as a normal part of their everyday lives has settled into a taken-for-granted understanding in Swedish courts. Prosecutors refer to the normalisation process when alleged victims change their stories, for example, or tell obvious lies during cross examinations.

This integration of a reality perspective within the legal frame has created a feeling rule for legal professionals – not to become angry when women change or retract their testimony. Overt displays of anger at victims in these cases have become rarer and restricted to backstage areas. In the extract below, Prosecutor Josefin, who specialises in IPV cases, received a call from a victim when she was sitting in the prosecutors' backstage room at court, preparing for trial in another IPV case:

> Prosecutor Josefin is on the phone and when she hangs up, she exclaims: "I *hate* these women who want to *withdraw their complaint*! Now she calls and says she wants me to drop the charges and I say, 'But he has *CONFESSED!*' (imitating the plaintiff's childish tone:) 'Yes, but *I'm the one* who reported him, and he doesn't want to *live with me* anymore.'" Prosecutor Anneli says thoughtfully, "It's difficult to put yourself in that living situation". Josefin agrees, but says it's still "*so HARD* that they *call and call and scream* that you should drop the charges."
>
> Prosecutor Josefin, 35+, and Prosecutor Anneli, 30+,
> fieldnotes prosecutor room in court, IPV, Sweden

In this situation, Prosecutor Josefin was in a safe backstage area with only her close colleagues in the intimate partner violence team present, making it possible to express non-respectable frustration at this particular victim and these victims in general ("I *hate* these women"). This is interesting in itself, since we only see these overt displays of anger with victims in intimate partner violence cases. The legal professionals do not express anger at victims of other types of abuse, or victims who have been fooled in fraud cases for example. But we can also note that the emotional "rule reminder" (Hochschild, 1979: 564), carefully expressed by Josefin's colleague Anneli ("It's difficult to put yourself in that living situation"), reminds Josefin that anger at victims is not accepted.[4]

Maintaining distance to moral outrage

While we have found these clear examples of moral outrage at defendants and moral disappointment at victims and witnesses, legal professionals in all our participating countries tend to reject moral anger. In legal systems founded on jury participation, the distance to moral outrage is protected by the judge, who limits the type of information that is provided to the jury. In legal systems with lay judges (often associated with the free evaluation of evidence), the professional judge instead polices the deliberations in order to exclude legally irrelevant assessments. This does not mean that judges (or juries and lay judges) are not driven by emotionally charged ideals of right and wrong. As has been described earlier, morality is instead linked to legal due process, rather than to the moral wrongdoing evident in the cases brought to court. Of course, defending due process hinges on actions that fall within the legal prerequisites, for example, when prosecutors and judges make a point of condemning the (illegal) *act* but not the *person*, a common type of statement that seems to function as a form of objectivity spell (Jacobsson, 2008) rather than a personal ethical position. The understanding and evaluation of the case should not be based on ideas of whether a person has behaved rightly and wrongly, but on whether the act includes the relevant prerequisites and whether the evidence holds beyond a reasonable doubt. In an elder abuse case in the United States, the defendants, who worked as carers, had been accused of mistreating their patient to such an extent that he eventually died from neglect, with untreated wounds filled with larvae. Prosecutor Julia thought that the defence lawyers had downplayed the severity of the case by repeatedly trying to get her to dismiss it, referring to their clients' moral

4 Due to the limited data available from Scotland, we lack data on these kinds of interactions. In the state from which our main United States data are collected, there is a strong policy on victims' rights, and prosecutors continuously talk to and check their planned investigatory routes and decisions with the victims in each case. We found very few anger outbursts directed at victims, but previous research indicate that legal professionals and other counsels express irritation and frustration towards uncomplying victims (Martin et al., 2008; Kolb, 2011).

standing in the community and lack of previous convictions. During a preparatory meeting at the prosecutors' office, the defence suddenly introduced a new piece of evidence:

> The defence lawyer picks up a journal and sits down again to show prosecutor Julia, saying that this is a day journal that the defendant kept to keep track of her daily errands that she did for the victim "and you're trying to say that they're *monsters*!" Prosecutor Julia [chuckles, dismissive tone] "no one says that they're monsters, it's my duty to look at the evidence."
>
> Prosecutor Julia, 30+, first instance court, fieldnotes prosecution office, elder abuse, USA

As this extract shows, the defence lawyers turned their strategy of referring to the moral standing of their clients back at the prosecutor, accusing her of basing her decisions on moral evaluations of the defendants' personality ("they're monsters"). Prosecutors generally consider such accusations reprehensible, as is indicated by Prosecutor Julia's chuckle, signalling that she takes the accusation as a joke. After the meeting, when the defence lawyer had left, she instead expressed outrage at what she interpreted as their disrespect: "This is what they're like! [throwing her arms out and shaking her head]".

Although the different legal settings examined incorporate different norms for expressing moral anger, as a general rule, the articulation of professional moral anger is not described as a balance between moral outrage and due process, but as moral outrage getting in the way of due process. However, as indicted by Prosecutor Julia's anger at the defence lawyers, morality, in the sense of getting the process right, is important, and as Solomon (1995: 242) has argued, builds on a "capacity for anger and outrage" if the rule of law is disrespected. The moral defence of due process, legal pathos, is a strong ideal for both prosecutors and judges, but its emotional expression is nonetheless guided by the legal norm of dispassion (Maroney, 2011), as indicated by Prosecutor Julia's chuckle and the way she repressed her anger emotions until the defence lawyers had left, thus giving her room for backstage venting. These interprofessional norms of emotional restraint between prosecutors and defence lawyers are also found among judges. While judges stress legal pathos when interacting with lay judges, we find that they are able to express their moral outrage more openly when judging on panels with other professional judges. Whether or not they display their anger, moral outrage can function as a signifier of irrelevant gut feelings that should not influence decisions or the assessment of complicated legal issues.

As depicted in Prosecutor Julia's case (and by Prosecutor Louise in Chapter 2, pages 36–38), prosecutors now and then need to defend their legal pathos from accusations from defence lawyers of acting on moral grounds (Wettergren and Bergman Blix, 2016). Among judges, their defence of due process is often made in response to lay expressions of justice that are guided by a moral, commonsensical, ideal. In the Swedish courts of first instance, where a professional judge rules with three lay judges, part of the judge's role as chair involves guarding against lay judges basing their evaluations on moral outrage. In the extract below, Judge Karin (45+, Sweden) is leading the panel's deliberations in a case of violence against a security guard. The defendant is a petite young woman on psychosis medication who had resisted being discharged from a psychiatric ward. When the guards had been called in, she had blood dripping from a venous catheter that had been removed and no shoes on her feet. The guards, who were tall and hefty, tried to take her out into the general waiting hall and she had allegedly kicked one of them on the knee while lying on her back on the floor. At the start of the judge's panel's deliberations, the court's clerk in training was asked to give her opinion, and had addressed the issue of credibility, stating that, "There is no reason for [the guards] to lie. It was an exercise of authority".

> Lay judge 3 becomes visibly upset and replies in a raised voice, gesticulating with her hands: "In essence, I can agree with that, but I think it is completely *absurd* to make such a *thing out of it*. She was *COMPLETELY DRUGGED*!" Lay judge 2 agrees, and in a calmer tone picks up the issue about the shoes. Judge Karin interrupts: "That [whether or not the defendant had shoes] has nothing to do with the matter. ...and at the same time, it is also the case that security guards must also be able to do their *job,* and it has become *common* for people to attack guards." She leans back in her chair, folding her arms across her chest. "You may think it is *unfortunate*, but [the defendant] is not so mentally ill that she cannot be held responsible for her actions." Lay judge 3 has calmed down a little, but remains engaged with the unfairness of the situation. Lay judge 2 jumps in: "Now we are *there*, how can we *help* her?" Judge Karin replies: "We have to convict her, but she can get probation." Karin looks at lay judge 3: "You can tell by looking at her that she [the defendant] is a fragile person." Lay judge 3 agrees in an upset tone: "That's the feeling you have as a layman, that there's so much that's *crazy* in the legal system!" Judge Karin turns to the clerk and reasons around the verdict for a while. When they have all agreed, she tells the lay judges: "You can have coffee for ten minutes", laughing a little. Everyone laughs a little as if to conclude with a good atmosphere.
>
> Judge Karin, 45+, first instance court, fieldnotes deliberation, violence against public servant, Sweden

The above case involved a rather ordinary assault case, with two guards as credible witnesses and an (intoxicated) defendant. From a legal point of view, the evaluation of guilt is straightforward, but the fact that the defendant was on medication for a psychosis, was not fully dressed, had blood dripping from her arm, and had a body half the size of the two male guards, made her role as perpetrator unconvincing from a commonsensical point of view. The foundational legal principle that people are capable of making free choices and are therefore responsible for their actions becomes muddled or even contradicted when a perpetrator so clearly demonstrates vulnerability and lacks power in relation to the victim.

The judge's immediate response is that these factors have "nothing to do with the matter". Her leaning back and folding her arms accentuates her distance to evaluations that are based on commonsensical and frustrated moral reasoning. Judge Karin interprets the lay judges' anger as being linked to the guards' decision to report the incident to the police, and she situates the guards' behaviour in relation to the heightened pressure experienced within the security occupations, as if to even out the power (im)balance between defendant and victim. In this way, Karin counters the lay judges' moral anger at the guards by highlighting the guards' moral right to perform their work without being attacked, as if balancing one moral rule against another. The way she sharply distances herself from allowing these issues to matter in relation to the evaluation of guilt is clearly separated from allowing them to matter in relation to sentencing, a separation that the lay judges immediately accept. Since guilt and sentencing are determined during the same deliberation, judges in Sweden (and Italy) need to safeguard this separation during deliberations with lay judges. Moral outrage should not influence judgements of guilt, but the cause of this moral outrage, the defendant being "a fragile person", is indeed relevant in relation to sentencing.

We can also note the low-key manner in which anger is displayed in the Swedish court setting. Voices are only marginally raised, there are few gestures (the lay judge gesticulating with her hands at the beginning), and when Judge Karin interrupts, the lay judges become silent, showing respect for Karin's status as a professional judge. Anger is evidenced by the lay judge's choice of words ("it is completely *absurd*"), engaged tone of voice, and multiple emphases (Retzinger, 1991). We can also note that Judge Karin, at the end of the deliberation, is careful not to let any feelings of upset leak into the next court case, laughing gently and offering the lay judges a break, thus restoring rapport and a good atmosphere.

Outrage as a clue

So far, Judge Karin's quick renunciation of moral outrage as a basis for evaluating guilt and making a ruling follows the expected professional route, with objective decisions being made without reference to emotional moral evaluations. However, when asked about this deliberation in a follow-up interview, Judge Karin described a more complex link between the lay judges' moral outrage and her legal evaluation:

> Well, I think it's good that they react ...and they are *right*, because I can also think that this person should not be in court. She is mentally ill,

> she has problems, and that meant that I had to go home and read about intent and so on to see if we really *could* convict her; but then I came to the conclusion, as I said preliminarily during the deliberation, that she was conscious *enough*, and what she said showed that she was aware of what was happening around her, and she got angry in various contexts, so she was conscious enough to be convicted. I think it's very important that they [the lay judges] can air this kind of thing. The problem is that they often think that things have the wrong reason. In this case, they were really angry with the security guards, but what happened was that the police were called to the scene, and they are the ones who registered a report; it was not the security guards themselves who wanted to convict her, so you kind of have to distinguish between the two, because I understood [the lay judges] to be upset about, 'why the hell should the security guards get her arrested, it's their job to take care of these people', but it's not certain that that was the case.
>
> Judge Karin, 45+, first instance court, post-deliberation interview, violence against public servant, Sweden

In this quote, we can see a difference compared to Judge Karin's earlier instant *display* of rejection ("nothing to do with the matter") and distance (leaning back and folding her arms) in response to the lay judges' anger, and her *experience* of insecurity in relation to the content of their arguments. While the lay judges' moral outrage appears to be linked to structural inequalities, such as an under-financed medical system that discharges people during a psychotic episode and a hierarchal gender system in which a woman may have good reason to panic when approached by two (large) men,[5] Karin's analysis is firmly grounded on the legal principle of individual accountability. Nevertheless, the lay judges' anger elevates Judge Karin's awareness of potential problems linked to the legal prerequisite of intent. Can a person who is experiencing a psychotic episode have the required intent to commit assault?[6] Karin believes that the lay judges' anger had been directed at the guards as individuals, and thinks that lay judges sometimes have "the wrong reasons", but their anger can nonetheless function as a useful indicator of a potential issue that the judge needs to consider. When asked specifically

5 Since lay judges in Sweden are selected from political parties, one might speculate that they may be prone to situate problems within institutional structures, since this fits with calls for political interventions.

6 Since 1965, the accountability requirement has no longer been part of the Swedish Criminal Code. A defendant suffering from a severe mental disorder or disability is prosecuted on the same grounds as a sane defendant, and potential adjustments are made at the sentencing stage. This differs from most countries, where accountability is viewed as a prerequisite for criminal liability. The suspension of the accountability requirement has complicated the assessment of intent in these cases, in particular with regard to the assessment of the defendant's subjective awareness of the situation and their actions. In general, the threshold for awareness is set very low and includes actions that are not purely reflexive.

about moral experience and legal reasoning, Judge Karin articulates how the lay judges' moral outrage can provide clues about her own taken-for-granted emotional evaluations:

> INTERVIEWER: But how do you experience this dialogue between the law and perceptions that this is right or wrong?
>
> JUDGE KARIN: Mm, but that's why they're [the lay judges] sitting there, because they're supposed to represent the people's opinion, and then it's my duty to bring them up to speed when it comes to the law, but I think it's-, it's a challenge in itself not to convince them, but to guide them in the law. And I mean, many of them are very competent and experienced, and it's useful for us to be forced to think, so you don't just act on your feeling, but if they ask a question, I have to manage to formulate a sensible answer.
>
> Judge Karin, 45+, first instance court, post-deliberation interview, violence against public servant, Sweden

From an emotional perspective, the most interesting part of this quote comes towards the end, when Judge Karin articulates that the lay judges' forceful articulations of their opinions force her, as a legal professional, not to act on her (legal gut) feeling. The lay judges' moral outrage serves to counteract routine feelings of confidence and certainty in applying the law to facts. The interaction forces the judge to articulate the legal prerequisites for the offence at issue and, in this case, the intentions of the law. Similar to the anger rippling from Henry Fonda's jury 8 to the rest of the jurors in the film *12 angry men*, the lay judges' moral outrage prompts Judge Karin's legal pathos. As she describes in the first part of the quote, and in line with the situation in jury trials, the professional judge needs to instruct the lay judges on legal issues without influencing their lay opinions. In contrast to jury trials, the interaction between lay and professional judges during deliberations may allow moral outrage in relation to particular issues, which forces professional judges to articulate their motivations in relation to the evaluation and judgement of a particular case.

In all the countries represented in our study, judges sit in panels in appellate courts, and in a few cases we did observe the airing of moral outrage even between professional judges during such deliberations.[7] In the example below from Italy, the three judges in a case of fraud (Judge Michela, Judge Giorgio, and Judge Flavia) expressed moral outrage at the defendants and at the ruling of the first instance judge at the start of the deliberation. They all

7 We do not have observational data from panel deliberations in the United States, only interviews, but the deliberative process in the one state in which we interviewed appeal judges involved less physical interaction, with draft judgments being circulated rather than judges actually sitting together.

expressed commonsensical convictions about who was guilty, while at the same time reproaching the first instance ruling for being commonsensical. The case involves four defendants: two care givers, a real estate agent, and a notary, all accused of having committed fraud against an elderly man. The first instance judge convicted the two care givers and the real estate agent, but acquitted the notary.

> JUDGE MICHELA: The real estate agent … I'm telling you now … in my opinion … he should be acquitted… the judge of the first instance who wrote the judgment talked of 'likelihood' …
>
> JUDGE GIORGIO: Never use those words in a judgment! EVER!
>
> JUDGE MICHELA: Here … let me read it to you… (judge of the first instance) says, '[The real estate agent] was the one who *likely* planned the whole thing' (…). I would actually convict the real estate agent, but I think he will be acquitted.
>
> JUDGE GIORGIO: I would convict the notary instead. They know pretty well how to draw up false deeds.
>
> JUDGE MICHELA: Do you have any doubts?
>
> JUDGE GIORGIO: Only that 'likely'. [They all laugh] Remember that it is *FORBIDDEN TO USE THIS EXPRESSION*!
>
> JUDGE FLAVIA: Just one doubt, why *THE HECK* didn't the most excellent [name of the judge of first instance] convict the notary as well? Also, the second real estate property had been evaluated by the judge; hence, the estate agent, who boasts of his 120 transactions a year, knew it!
>
> JUDGE GIORGIO: The two youngsters [care givers] have disinherited the relatives in a despicable manner. Now, let us probe all the hypotheses…
>
> Judges Giorgio, 65+, Michela, 55+, Flavia 60+, appellate court, fieldnotes deliberation, fraud, Italy

In this interaction, the judges' moral convictions about guilt refer to 'gut feelings' (cf. Minissale, 2024) based on stereotypical understandings of the roles involved (notaries know how to draw up false deeds, the boastful real estate agent knew what was going on). These displays are somewhat sarcastic ("They know pretty well") but expressed in a rather good mood, whereas the indignation towards the first instance judge generates moral outrage ("it is forbidden!", "why the heck!"). It may seem contradictory that, while expressing their own subjective values, the appellate court judges so forcefully distance themselves from the subjective values of the first instance judge, but the key is found in Judge Giorgio's final sentence: "Now, let us probe all the hypotheses…". In this way, the judges' moral outrage towards the defendants may serve as a caution, that they need to articulate their own moral convictions and to either discard them or evaluate their legal legitimacy in a more systematic manner by 'probing' into the actions of the different actors. The fault of the first instance judge was thus not her subjective conviction per se, but her having stopped with her subjective evaluation and not put it to the test, as indicated by her choice of the word 'likelihood'. To the judges, the use of this word in a ruling signals inexperience or a lack of diligence and thus elicits strong reactions, since it opens up for criticism at the appeal stage, forcing the appeal judges to deal with the matter.

As with the case involving Judge Karin above, moral outrage can offer clues for identifying weak points in an evaluation. In contrast to the Swedish case, the Italian judges expressed their indignation more openly at the start of the deliberation whereas Judge Karin aired hers in an interview at which only the researcher was present. The Italian judges are all professional judges and have been colleagues for several years. Giorgio is the head of the panel and therefore guides the discussion ("let's probe all the hypotheses") by inviting the others to participate. They are more open to showing their stereotype-based gut feelings and to using vernacular expressions, which signals that they trust one another's ability to ensure that these expressions do not get in the way of their legal expertise. Even if they express their emotions in a low-key manner, they are more emotionally expressive than their Swedish counterparts, continuously gesticulating with their hands while talking, and more clearly raising the pitch and volume of their voices to make a point. This more expressive emotional regime is also evidenced by the fact that the deliberation was attended by three trainee students, in addition to the researcher, and the judges nonetheless displayed their moral outrage relatively freely in front of this audience. For the Italian judge, moral outrage at the beginning of the deliberation is not prohibited and may be used as a starting point for legal evaluation.

Retribution versus recognition – paths of moral anger

As we saw in the previous section, legal professionals distance themselves from evaluations that are based on moral outrage, but they also use moral outrage as a guide to the need for further examination, turning anger into a dynamic driver of epistemic inquiry. In this section, we will continue to look at anger as an initiator of action, either in the form of retribution or being resolute. Martha Nussbaum (2016) defines anger as constituting both backward and forward evaluation: this bad thing happened and I do not want it to happen again. She argues that the forward-looking part can be divided into three logics: regaining status, payback, or making it better, of which the first two are similar in that they include retaliation in some form, either to regain one's own status by lowering the status of the other, or to exact revenge. A study on prosecutorial emotions in Israel (Leiterdorf-Shkedy and Gal, 2019) found anger to serve as a forward-looking form of moral engagement in justice, with prosecutors being proud of their anger. They used it as an engine to drive retaliation during both preliminary investigations and cross-examinations in court, but the researchers also found that the positive associations linked to anger also functioned as a cover for other feelings, such as compassion for victims or pity for defendants. In our data, the link between anger and retribution was rare, but we have a few instances where anger was explicitly linked to punitive decisions. In the extract below, Prosecutor Charlotte (45+, USA) talks about an upcoming case in which she wants to revoke bail for a vehicular homicide in which the defendant drove into the victim's car:

> [determined tone] "I want to *lock him up*! The poor man [the victim] suffered for five months... it was *horrific*." She pauses for a moment and then says [judgemental tone] "you know when two thugs starts shooting and killing that's *one* thing, this case... [voice softens] this man had *parked*, checking his phone and the defendant had *no* drivers licence. The victim's car was *totally destroyed*, he's *dying* and the [defendant] RUNS! Now he's on GPS, he's *all* over the damn place. Trying to get the bond revoked, the Judge yelled at him and he's *still not in compliance*! ... [her voice is trembling and she speaks with force behind each word] I'm gonna ask for his bond to be *revoked* and him to be *locked up* pending trial. I'm just over it. The man was *completely smashed* and he *ran*. [Defendant's name] makes me so mad!"
>
> Prosecutor Charlotte, 45+, first instance court,
> fieldnotes shadowing, vehicular homicide, USA

This quote is interesting because it breaks certain foundational feeling rules that are included in the prosecutorial role. Prosecutor Charlotte differentiates between victims of different value, where 'a thug' is not as deserving of legal justice as the ideal victim (Christie, 1986) in this case. Her rage at the defendant intensifies when she compares the respectability of the victim, who had stopped his car before looking at his phone, with the actions of the defendant, who did not have a driver's licence, ran from the crash scene, and did not subordinate himself to the angry judge. In this way, Charlotte's anger comes from a moral evaluation of the defendant's actions both at the crime scene and in court. On the one hand, her statement is inconsistent with an objective evaluation that does not distinguish between victims of crime in terms of moral value, and that demonstrates an interest focused on criminal acts rather than despicable ones. On the other hand, the defendant's actions may be linked to a risk for recidivism, which is important when deciding on bail. What stands out is that Charlotte openly links her outrage to a legally grounded decision, and that she degrades the status of the defendant. The defendant is unworthy of her professional respect (Barnett and Mann, 2013) and should submit to the higher-status judge. Her evaluation seems to be based more on moral than legal authority. This is also the case when Judge Blake (60+, USA) became angry when a defendant failed to show up in court for her hearing. When the defence lawyer informed Judge Blake that she could not find the defendant, Blake exclaimed:

> "I promise I'm gonna have her ARRESTED!" He points to the witness awaiting the hearing and says [disapproving tone], "*He* shouldn't be dragged out here several times if *she* can't show up." The defence lawyer says that she is going to go look for her. Judge Blake instead shouts at another defence lawyer, calling her by her name and asking if she is ready; she is standing in the doorway and shouts back, "*I'M TALKING TO MY CLIENT!*" Her voice is sharp, and Blake asks her what she's been up to, and she tells him that she's been in conversation with a witness. Judge Blake gets annoyed and says, "I'll see you at 3." He won't hear her case until then. She turns around and stomps out of court. Judge Blake mutters, "If she's left knowing that we were gonna have this hearing I'm gonna..."
>
> Judge Blake, 60+, first instance court, IPV, USA

In this exchange Judge Blake motivates his anger by referring to the witness, who has shown up in court in vain ("*He* shouldn't be dragged out here"). Blake's anger spreads to the next lawyer in turn, who refuses to accept his unsolicited anger and shouts back. Judge Blake continues his outpour of anger and postpones the lawyer's hearing until later, and returns to the earlier case, muttering general threats at the defendant. As in the earlier case involving Prosecutor Charlotte, Judge Blake's threat of arrest may be linked to legal grounds, since failing to show up in court can result in arrest to ensure that the hearing takes place. However, these legal grounds are accompanied by a retaliatory delivery ("I promise I'm gonna have her ARRESTED!") and the motivation of his decision as relating to the defendant's potential lack of respect for the court ("If she's left knowing that we were gonna have this hearing I'm gonna...") signalling an effort to regain moral, rather than legal, authority.

In these examples, the judges' retaliatory actions or threats are initiated on the basis of moral outrage at the defendant. One could speculate that the judge's more active role in common law compared to (adversarial) civil law systems invites this type of fast, responsive initiative, based on immediate emotional reactions. In Sweden, judges are expected to be more passive, and it is not unusual for prosecutors and lawyers to complain about judges who do not react or who react too slowly to incidents in the courtroom. In one unusual example, Judge Monica (45+, Sweden) acted on her moral outrage when a witness had been served to attend a robbery trial, but had called the court to say that he did not intend to come. Both the prosecutor and the defence wanted to examine this witness, and Judge Monica decided on a break so that they could try to contact him by phone:

> When everyone has left the room, the clerk dials the witness's number and hands over the phone to Judge Monica. They talk for a while, but

> the witness does not seem to come around and Monica exclaims: "As I *said*, I'll *say it again*, it's still not something you can decide for *yourself!*" When the call is over Monica turns directly to the clerk, articulating every word: "Phone number for the officer on duty; we'll bring him in immediately". She explains that he said [mimicking obstinate tone]: "I don't have time to talk to you anymore," and hung up. When she has been connected to the police, she asks in a friendly tone, "Do you think you have time to pick him up right away?" Before calling the parties back in, Judge Monica turns to the lay judges who have been on a coffee break and says, "We sent the police to the witness's home; he was so stupid on the phone". One lay judge replies, "Some people have to be put in their place." Judge Monica replies in the affirmative. The clerk calls the parties back in. After the hearing, when only the judges' panel remains in the room, a lay judge asks about the witness who didn't want to come, and Monica replies, "Since they have made one unsuccessful attempt to pick him up, they can now request that they pick him up 6 hours before the rescheduled trial" She emphasizes to the court clerk that, "They should *not* call him this time. Speak to a clerk and tell them that this is *urgent*. They will have to put it out *at once*. The witness must absolutely *not be called*, he must be *collected*."
>
> Judge Monika, 45+, first instance court,
> fieldnotes break in hearing, robbery, Sweden

Judge Monica's anger is similar to Judge Blake's anger above: both got angry at the failure of a defendant or witnesses to show up in court. The defendant/witness' lack of respect wastes court time, costs money, and in effect obstructs justice. The difference between the two provides clues about the diverging emotional regimes of the United States and Sweden, in that Judge Blake openly expressed his anger frontstage, whereas Judge Monica did not show her anger in the open court. Her anger, displayed backstage, was backgrounded to a large extent, paving the way for her lines of action. This can be seen in her reasoning with the witness on the phone ("As I *said*, I'll *say it again*, it's still not something you can decide for *yourself*"), and also in her resolute decision to call the police. In contrast to Judge Blake, whose anger spread to a lawyer who happened to be in the room, Judge Monica had a friendly tone when talking to the police for assistance in picking him up, while continuing the hearing as if nothing had happened. Her anger makes her energetic and she seems to enjoy the feeling; she is cheerful in her anger, demonstrating determination rather than retaliation.

The backstage outlet for complaining about unruly defendants or witnesses was also found in a judge panel in Italy, where the judges disagreed about mitigating circumstances in a case of IPV and rape. Whether or not to give the maximum sentencing reduction via generic mitigating circumstances is almost like a mathematical operation, but judicial discretion can result in a reduction of up to one-third of the sentence. In this case, Judge Sonia voted for maximum reduction, while Beatrice and Enrico disagreed:

> ENRICO: We're borderline, eh... Therefore, do we give him the maximum reduction or not?
>
> BEATRICE: Of what, general mitigating circumstances? In my opinion, not giving them to him in full is ok.
>
> SONIA [decisive tone]: *Come on*, he has always been present and good.
>
> BEATRICE [irritated tone]: With all the nonsense he has told us, I see it more unfavourably.
>
> Judge Enrico, 60+, Judge Beatrice, 50+, Judge Sonia, 45+, first instance court, fieldnotes deliberation, IPV and rape, Italy

Beatrice's anger at the defendant's behaviour during the trial makes her prone not to reduce his sentence in the standardised way. The defendant in Italy (and in Sweden) has the right to remain silent or lie in his defence, but as depicted in earlier quotes (page 71), judges dislike obvious lying from defendants and plaintiffs alike, since they see it as signalling disrespect for the court. Judge Beatrice's reluctance to reduce the sentence could be interpreted as a retaliatory reaction to the defendant's behaviour, but falls within the judges' discretion when taking general mitigating circumstances into account, since these can include remorse.

While the United States examples, although few in appearance, demonstrated strong retaliatory aims, these civil law examples rather illustrate determination to 'put it right' or a subtle taste of retributive wishes. However, we find delayed and slightly more open forms of retaliation towards other legal professionals in Sweden and Italy. These take the form of status degradations, in written rulings, such as when a ruling in a fraud case stated that the indictment was "evidently" not proven. A hint from the judge which generated both anger and shame, as indicated by the prosecutor not mentioning this to any of her colleagues, and by her long explanation and venting of this issue during a follow-up interview "well it doesn't feel very nice..." (Prosecutor Elsa, 50+, fraud, Sweden). But moral outrage can also be combined with legal pathos in line with Judge Monica's reaction, which did not generate revenge but rather a relentless effort to make the witness do what he was required to do, which was to come to court and testify.

As indicated in these last examples, the expectation of an active or passive judge might influence the way revenge is expressed in front stage or backstage regions, but it does not seem to be the immediacy of the reaction in itself that prompts the focus on revenge. The common idea of anger as an uncontrolled emotion that boils over into instant retaliation does not fit with the status degradation of Prosecutor Elsa that was expressed in the written ruling weeks after the trial. Nor did Judge Monica's prompt actions when the witness could not be bothered to show up appear retaliatory, but rather a means of resolutely unclogging the machinery of justice (to paraphrase Judge Rossella's earlier quote). One potential clue here is found in Prosecutor Elsa's interpretation of the judge's status degradation as a roundabout way of reprimanding the prosecutors' office as a whole for filing too many poorly substantiated indictments in this particular type of case. She, in turn, thought that the police were to blame for not providing them with sufficiently well-conducted investigations. In this way, retaliation became a (rather inefficient) way to direct attention at problems in the way justice is organised. When we look at interprofessional moral anger more closely, weaknesses in the law or the organisation of law come to the fore.

Shame and resignation – moving away from anger

As demonstrated in earlier chapters, interprofessional anger in court is common, and demonstrates the interdependence of legal professionals in performing their roles in line with demands for objectivity, impartiality, and independence (Bergman Blix and Wettergren, 2019; Roach Anleu and Mack, 2021). Interprofessional anger may come from individual resentment towards a specific person for being sloppy, manipulative, or just unreliable in general (see further Chapter 2). As we will focus on in this last section, interprofessional anger, although directed at an individual in the moment, may reveal weaknesses in the legislation or in legal procedure, where the discrepancy between the intention of the law and legal practice becomes too wide. Here, interprofessional moral anger indicates frustration over the law failing to do justice.

As depicted in the example of Prosecutor Elsa, interprofessional anger in court can express itself in the form of status degradation. Status degradation may also be expressed in the other direction, from a prosecutor towards the court or the judge. In this next case, Prosecutor Sara (35+, Sweden), describes how she became angry when a trial was cancelled because a defendant had not shown up for the trial yet again, thinking, "What kind of fucking *system* is that?" Just like Prosecutor Charlotte, who referred to people involved in criminal activities as "thugs", Prosecutor Sara talks in derogatory terms about the defendant as being [annoyed tone] "some junkie who didn't *come* of course", connoting stereotypical notions related to class, race, and gender. However, Sara's moral outrage is not directed at the individual himself, but at the court who "could have calculated that *before*, and could have *cancelled* the case too, BEFORE. BUT THEY DIDN'T", accusing the court of placing case processing goals over the inconvenience experienced by the people who are called to attend court. She decided to act:

> And then I thought 'Should *I* have to stand for this?' So what I did [laughs], even though I probably understood that it wasn't going to *work*, I said to the associate judge 'Yes [clicks tongue], I'm asking for him to be detained, in absentia... *now*'. And she just said 'Well, well, well, but he

> hasn't been served,' and so on. I just said, 'Well, you see how things look here; everyone is here, except him, and it's been cancelled before; there's no way it will be decided unless he's in custody, so I'm asking for him to be detained now in absentia.' And so on, but she didn't dare to detain him. Although I still thought I had a moral victory in that she had to announce that she wasn't detaining him in front of all the people she had forced to come... so, I thought...[laughter] 'Well, now you can fucking stand for it, so if you're going to be that *defensive* it's a JUDGMENT; if you're going to be so defensive then you can probably be, but then you have to sit there and stand for that in front of all the people as well.'
>
> Prosecutor Sara, 35+, first instance court, interview, Sweden

Here, the legal procedural rationale of being served, and of not being subject to any repercussions if the court has failed to deliver the summons, is contrasted with the moral rationale of wasting people's time and the state's money. Prosecutor Sara's anger was reinforced by the fact that several of the other people who had come for the trial had expressed their anger at yet another postponement. Prosecutor Sara gets annoyed at the court's naivety and specifically points out that the trial was led by a judge in training (associate judge). It is unlikely that she would have reacted in the same way if the chair had been a senior high-status judge (cf. Lively and Powell, 2006). But here, her status degradation of the judge feels like a moral victory; she sets out to make the judge feel ashamed in having to stand by her (legally correct but cowardly) decision. Prosecutor Sara's moral anger, which led to her unusual request to detain the defendant, points towards a custom in Swedish court procedure that people should not be detained or collected in order to attend court until all other options have been tried several times. The law does not prohibit a more active approach, but this is seldom used, and a judge in training, who is dependent on good reviews from senior colleagues, would make herself vulnerable to criticism if she stood in the vanguard to bring about change.[8] Prosecutor Sara's moral anger points towards a more general conflict between prosecutors as active defenders of the law and judges who are passive, and at the legal system's slow turnaround times and bureaucratic procedures. This lower-status associate judge had to take the hit.

We also find instances where anger relates to moral accusations of non-objective decision making by judges or prosecutors, or unprofessional or lazy work by defence lawyers. Prosecutors express moral complaints about defence lawyers in all of the countries examined. They "are only in it for the money", "they don't make an effort", "they choose the easiest way out", "they focus more on performing loyalty to their client rather than actually

8 In the few instances in our data where the judge has determined that a defendant or witness who has not shown up should be collected, as in the example of Judge Monica on pages 83–84, all have been senior judges with a reputation for having an active judging style.

being loyal", "they lie", "they attack the prosecutor personally in court to win a case or accuse them of failing in their objectivity", accusations that have been noted in several studies (Törnqvist, 2017; Bergman Blix and Wettergren, 2018; Flower, 2020). In the example below, Prosecutor Nicola (55+, Italy) is upset at the defence lawyer for hurting her client as a result of sloppy defence work in two cases of sexual violence:

> The public defence lawyer should have suggested to him to confess...So if the two proceedings would have been re-united, his sentence would have been less severe. However, since he will be convicted, he will get 6.5 years and 2.5 years. She defended him *very badly*; she did not even visit him in prison, because she would only have received 60 € from the state... Also, this lawyer was a VPO [Vice-Procuratore Onorario, a lawyer who temporarily works as a public prosecutor], SO EVEN WORSE! Even more *serious*! [angry tone] She is part of an institution WHICH I ALSO REPRESENT! Really an obtuse stupidity - *times two*! She is not working in her client's interest.
>
> Prosecutor Nicola, 55+, first instance court, post-hearing interview, sexual violence, Italy

In this quote, Prosecutor Nicola gets angry at the defence lawyer's lack of moral responsibility. The defence lawyer had not given her client relevant advice, she had not worked to reduce his sentence, and she had not even visited him in prison. Nicola's moral outrage is interlaced with professional shame as a result of the defence lawyer's prior affiliation with the prosecutors' office ("She is part of an institution WHICH I ALSO REPRESENT!"). In a way that is similar to Prosecutor Sara's outrage at the judge described above, Nicola (in this case implicitly) acknowledges that the defence lawyer had not broken any procedural rules, having acted within the limits of the law, but both Sara and Nicola accuse the judge and defence lawyer respectively of not interpreting and acting on the intentions of the law – the associate judge because she was a coward, the defence lawyer because she only had her eyes on the money. As described earlier, civil law systems 'apply law', a task that is associated with a rather mechanical procedure (Remiche, 2015), but these examples demonstrate that legal professionals harbour expectations that part of being a legal professional involves taking account of a wider interpretation of the intentions of the law in their daily legal practice. These instances are interesting in that Sara and Nicola's anger points to taken-for-granted applications of the law that show its vulnerability to cautious (or as Sara would have it cowardly) or manipulative (or as Nicola argues disloyal) behaviour and decisions.

The legal professionals also sometimes expressed moral outrage at the failure of other institutions to live up to moral standards. One example occurred when a victim, who was being examined in court, described that she had repeatedly failed to report a crime to the police because the police did not answer the phone: "The judge says that he found it 'scary' to hear her story about trying to call the police. He shakes his head and says, 'A personal opinion again' and quickly looks at the researcher." (Judge Konrad, 55+, Sweden). This might seem like a rather innocent and fair display of moral outrage, but as the quick look at the researcher demonstrates, judges in Sweden experience high demands to refrain from moral evaluations. In Italy, we found examples in which judges applied mitigating circumstances to adjust what they considered to be unfair consequences of applying the law in the correct way, such as when a son with a complicated parental relationship and a horrible upbringing was found guilty of abusing his mother. Just as Judge Karin had in the case involving the psychotic woman, these Italian judges tried to strike a balance between legal and moral legitimacy.

However, when Swedish legal professionals get angry as a result of experiencing a discrepancy between their moral and legal evaluations, their anger often leads to resignation. In the case below, Judge Amanda (30+, Sweden), feels strongly that the victim's (extended family's) right to compensation for damages in a murder trial is much lower than it should be:

> [thoughtfully, slowly] Sometimes you can feel a little bit stingy. So, it's clear that I *personally* can think that 'Yes, but IT's CLEAR... it's CLEAR he should HAVE some MONEY' [ending slowly]. He gave a nice impression and *very* committed and ... From a kind of *moral* level, I would probably THINK that 'YES, but ... he should probably HAVE.' [...] When I read up on it and we also *finally* came to the conclusion that ... IT REQUIRES SOMETHING VERY *SPECIAL*... And it... [resigned] it wasn't in this case [end resigned]. [...] [thoughtfully] But... [irritated] yes, it can... it's *not* always you get, get the *outcome* that you would *feel* GOOD about in your heart, but that, *that's* what it's all about *too*, being able to distance yourself from it.
>
> Judge Amanda, 30+, appellate court,
> post-hearing interview, murder, Sweden

Judge Amanda expresses a feeling of displeasure and anger at having to be "stingy", not being able to decide on the compensation that she would feel to be fair. Her outrage is articulate and directed at the law in a clearly personal voice, with emphasis placed on words and a raised voice; she would want to compensate more, but the rules are restrictive. She also continuously tries to distance herself from her anger, her tone shifting between anger, thoughtfulness, and resignation, and also shifting between the singular and collective personal pronoun (I/we). Judge Amanda's reflections on her moral outrage eventually led to feelings of resignation. Her moral outrage does not result in any change of behaviour or decision in the moment, as in previous examples involving revenge or recognition, but leads to a sense of moral responsibility to give up, to distance herself from moral outrage in order to align herself with demands for legal pathos and dispassion. We only found these clear expressions of moral outrage leading to resignation in our Swedish data. On the one hand, they are in line with the high demands placed on legal dispassion in the Swedish courts by comparison with other countries (Wettergren and Bergman Blix, 2021). On the other, they shed light on demands to carefully delink legal pathos from moral outrage in a way that we did not observe in the other countries. In comparison, our findings from Italy either show efforts to use the law to handle perceived unfairness, such as deploying mitigating or aggravating circumstances, or displayed contentment from following the law. Here, moral outrage and legal pathos are carefully integrated or completely decoupled.

References

Barnett Georgia and Mann Ruth E. (2013) Empathy deficits and sexual offending: A model of obstacles to empathy. *Aggression and Violent Behavior* 18: 228–239.

Bergman Blix Stina. (2015) Professional emotion management as a rehearsal process. *Professions and Professionalism* 5: 1–15.

Bergman Blix Stina and Wettergren Åsa. (2018) *Professional Emotions in Court: A Sociological Perspective*. London: Routledge.

Bergman Blix Stina and Wettergren Åsa. (2019) The emotional interaction of judicial objectivity. *Oñati Socio-Legal Series* 9: 726–746.

Bourdieu Pierre. (1986) The force of law: Toward a sociology of the juridical field. *The Hastings Law Journal* 38: 814–853.

Christie Nils. (1986) The ideal victim. In: EA Fattah (ed) *From Crime Policy to Victim Policy: Reorienting the Justice System*. Basingstoke: Springer, 17–30.

Deflem Mathieu. (2008) *Sociology of Law - Visions of a Scholarly Tradition*, Cambridge: Cambridge University Press.

Dworkin Ronald. (1986) *Law's Empire*. Cambridge: Harvard University Press.

Field Stewart and Tata Cyrus. (2023) *Criminal Justice and the Ideal Defendant in the Making of Remorse and Responsibility*. Oxford: Bloomsbury Publishing.

Flower Lisa. (2020) *Interactional Justice: The Role of Emotions in the Performance of Loyalty*. Abingdon, Oxon: Routledge.

Frodlund Åsa. (2002) *Sju ungdomar om sin rättegång (Seven Young People About Their Trial)*. Stockholm: Swedish National Council for Crime Prevention (Brottsförebyggande rådet).

Hochschild Arlie Russell. (1979) Emotion work, feeling rules, and social structure. *American Journal of Sociology* 85: 551–575.

Jacobsson Katarina. (2008) "We can't just do it any which way": Objectivity work among Swedish prosecutors. *Qualitative Sociology Review* IV: 46–68.

Johansen Louise Victoria and Laursen Julie. (2023) Moral Communication in Court. In: L Flower and S Klosterkamp (eds) *Courtroom Ethnography: Exploring Contemporary Approaches, Fieldwork and Challenges*. Cham: Palgrave Macmillan, 161–177.

Kolb Kenneth. (2011) Sympathy work: Identity and emotion management among victim-advocates and counselors. *Qualitative sociology* 34: 101–119.

Leiterdorf-Shkedy Shira and Gal Tali. (2019) The sensitive prosecutor: Emotional experiences of prosecutors in managing criminal proceedings. *International Journal of Law and Psychiatry* 63: 8–17.

Lerner Jennifer S, Li Ye, Valdesolo Piercarlo, et al. (2015) Emotion and decision making. *Annual review of psychology* 66: 799–823.

Lively Kathryn J and Powell Brian (2006) Emotional expression at work and at home: Domain, status, or individual characteristics? *Social Psychology Quarterly* 69: 17–38.

Maroney Terry A. (2011) The persistent cultural script of judicial dispassion. *California Law Review* 99: 629–681.

Maroney Terry A. (2012) Angry judges. *Vanderbilt Law Review* 65: 1207–1286.

Patricia Martin Y, Schrock Douglas, Leaf Margaret and Carmen von Rohr. (2008) Rape work: Emotional dilemmas in work with victims. In: S Fineman (ed) *The Emotional Organization: Passions and Power*. New York: Wiley-Blackwell, 44–60.

Minissale Alessandra. (2023) *Emotions in Legal Decisions: The Construction of Objective Narratives in Italian Criminal Trials*. PhD thesis. Department of Sociology, Uppsala University, Uppsala.

Minissale Alessandra. (2024) Scrutinizing gut feelings: Emotional reflexive practices in Italian courts. *Emotions and Society* 6: 7–25.

Nussbaum Martha C. (2016) *Anger and Forgiveness: Resentment, Generosity, Justice*. Oxford: Oxford University Press.

Remiche Adélaïde. (2015) When judging is power: A gendered perspective on the French and American judiciaries. *Journal of Law and Courts* 3: 95–113.

Retzinger Suzanne M. (1991) *Violent Emotions: Shame and Rage in Marital Quarrels*. London: Sage Publications.

Roach Anleu Sharyn and Mack Kathy. (2021) *Judging and Emotion: A Socio-legal Analysis*. Abingdon, Oxon: Routledge.

Scheff Thomas J. (1990) Socialization of emotions: Pride and shame as causal agents. In: TD Kemper (ed) *Research Agendas in the Sociology of Emotions*. New York: State University of New York Press, 281–305.

Solomon Robert C. (1995) *A Passion for Justice: Emotions and the Origins of the Social Contract*. Lanham: Rowman & Littlefield.

Tausch Nicole, Becker Julia C, Spears Russell, et al. (2011) Explaining radical group behavior: Developing emotion and efficacy routes to normative and nonnormative collective action. *Journal of personality and social psychology* 101: 129–148.

Tyler Tom R and Bies Robert J. (1990) Beyond Formal Procedures: The interpersonal context of procedural justice. In: JS Carroll (ed) *Applied Social Psychology and Organizational Settings*. London: Psychology Press, 77–98.

Törnqvist Nina. (2017) Att göra rätt. En studie om professionell respektabilitet, emotioner och narrativa linjer bland relationsvåldsspecialiserade åklagare (Doing just right: A study on professional respectability, emotions and narrative lines among prosecutors specialised in relationship violence). PhD thesis. Department of Criminology, Stockholm University, Stockholm.

Weber Max. (1998) Bureaucracy. In: HH Gerth and CW Mills (eds) *From Max Weber: Essays in Sociology*. New York: Routledge, 196–244.

Wettergren Åsa and Bergman Blix Stina. (2016) Empathy and objectivity in the legal process: The case of Swedish prosecutors. *Journal of Scandinavian Studies in Criminology and Crime Prevention* 17: 19–35.

Wettergren Åsa and Bergman Blix Stina. (2021) Comparing culturally embedded frames of judicial dispassion. In: S Bandes, JL Madeira, K Temple and E Kidd White (eds) *Research Handbook on Law and Emotion*. Northampton, MA: Edward Elgar Publishing, 146–163.

5 Discussion

Anger comes to life in the friction between means and ends in legal professional life. In this book, we explored the *rationales* behind legal anger, its logic and origins, drawing on the perspectives of judges and prosecutors in Italy, Sweden, the United States, and Scotland.

Etymologically, the word *rationality* comes from Latin, and involves a somewhat tautological merging of 'calculation' and 'reason'. Rationality implies the use of conscious, logical, and meticulous actions to reach goals. It also signifies the importance of the power of deduction and an agile ability to move our thinking through a persistent web of contradictions and brief intuitions. Rational behaviours help us overcome immediate problems and achieve long-term goals. When we instead speak of irrational behaviours, imprudence, detrimental, and irresoluteness come to mind. In many ways, anger epitomises emotionality, and by extension, irrationality. However, we argue that the unsettling character of anger, by directing our attention to a problem, also gives it a problem-solving quality – and a rationality of its own. The French expression *esprit d'escalier* (stairway spirit) illustrates this lingering role of anger in not letting go of a problem (even though the crushing reply comes too late).

If we abandon the idea of rationality as something universal and temporally infinite, we may ask ourselves how rationality and rational anger unfold in court. As is the case with knowledge (Haraway, 1988; Harding, 1992), rationality is always bounded (Simon, 1990; Jones, 1999), tangled up in time and place, located in the vantage point of the present situation. According to Weber, rationality creates patterns in relationships, and ever since his seminal work, modern societies and their institutions, law among them, have been viewed as being characterised by the dominance of a rationality cultivated in bureaucratic settings (Kalberg, 1980; Deflem, 2008). In his understanding of law, Weber emphasises the difference between substantive and formal rationalisation, where the former involves clusters of values that guide actions, while the latter involves a purposive form of conduct in which the importance of means and correct procedure exceeds that of the actual ends. Law is aligned with substantive rationality when legal practices are trying to achieve an ultimate justice, 'directing' law towards more general ethical and

DOI: 10.4324/9781003330592-5

normative values in society. In parallel, formal law is produced when legal decisions are solely made on the facts of the case, promoting homogeneity and predictability, rather than being motivated by certain value-related ends. Weber's distinction between the two forms of rationality that inform law are tangential to 'ideal types', and the judges and prosecutors in this study illustrate the presence of a dynamic interface between formal and substantive rationalities, as their anger is entwined with different obstacles to the performance of correct procedure as well as being allied with the achievement of legally sound outcomes and the mirroring of wider societal values.

As a point of departure, we argued that legal anger occupies a special space in the legal realm, paradoxically residing at both the periphery and the very centre of legal practices and ideas. This ubiquitous yet fleeting space makes anger a unique feature in the world of legal emotions, and this tension is a fascinating topic in itself. This final chapter recaps the study's major findings, probing deeper into the comparisons between the countries examined. We then turn our gaze to the interconnectedness of emotions and discuss how legal anger becomes entangled and interspersed with other emotions such as surprise, patience, and sympathy. Next, we come back to the question that has echoed throughout the book – what is rational in anger? Lastly, we take a step back to expound on how legal anger is linked to larger cultural and social structures. For the impatient reader, if there is one takeaway from this book, it is that anger serves many functions in the courtroom and its rationality must be understood in relation to situation and perspective. With all the imaginable caveats, anger like other emotions is adaptive and we therefore need to focus on what it *does* rather than what it essentially *is*.

Feeling the same and feeling different

Looking at what legal professionals get angry about, how their anger unfolds temporally and adapts to legal tasks and problems, and how anger balances between legal pathos, the promotion of a just process, and moral outrage, the condemnation of offences, we find foundational similarities across our four countries. Legal professionals in Sweden, Italy, the United States, and Scotland all care about the narratives told in court being made fit for legal evaluation and assessment. They all get angry when lay people talk about the 'wrong things', in the 'wrong ways' and at the 'wrong time', or when other legal professionals present unfocused or twisted narratives, and they all use anger as capital (Nordquist and Bergman Blix, 2022) to enforce complicity.

Legal anger signals that narratives, in the eyes of the legal professionals, are vague, inefficient, confusing, or unfair, stressing the high demands for exactitude and precision in legal language and assessments. While judges and prosecutors have the status margin required to employ anger as a tool, their efforts to draw the line between relevant and irrelevant information are not always easy and they try to balance expressions of anger with patience and other forms of anger management. When legal professionals try to manage their anger or regret their angry displays in retrospect, they admit that overly elaborated or messy narratives are sometimes required to evaluate the credibility of stories or to enable the lay people involved to talk about at times traumatic events during public examinations. Even so, demands for precisely demarcated stories about an often-complex reality firmly steer the representation of reality in court, since the overly elaborated telling of 'true' stories confuses and muddles the information needed to make legally correct decisions. Demarcated narratives bring ease and relief to legal professionals because they rhyme well with the legal method of encoding and assessment (Bergman Blix and Minissale, 2022), but such aesthetic simplifications also involve a risk of misinterpreting a complicated and messy reality. This anger logic is present in all the countries represented in our data.

In all countries, legal professionals talk about and manifest efforts to manage their anger when it gets in the way of their work, but in many situations, it is not the anger itself that is managed but the situation or legal problem. Anger surfaces when it is appropriate to the situation, sometimes backstage as a vent and sometimes frontstage as a tool. Anger surfaces in short and intense outbursts, simmers as a low-key energiser, or is performed to indicate status. In this way, anger adapts both temporally and spatially to legal tasks and ideals (Goffman, 1959). This indicates that legal professionals do not have to devote energy to appraising their anger in efforts to manage it, but can instead direct their focus at managing the problem that has the potential to make them angry. Although the legal sphere abides by an ideal of dispassion, where anger can signal loss of control and reason, legal professionals with high levels of power and status can often break with these norms without incurring costs (Scarduzio, 2011), especially when their breaches of feeling rules are linked to demands for correct legal procedure.

From a theoretical point of view, it is interesting to note that when legal professionals need to solve a legal problem, they not only refrain from expressing anger but also show no sign of feeling it, as though the task at hand closes the door to this feeling in the moment. This indicates that when high status makes anger acceptable, it can be put aside without much ado until a suitable time occurs. Adding a temporal perspective to the analysis of professional anger points to two issues that are important to developing our understanding of anger: Firstly, our findings support the view that the ability to align anger with the situation at hand not only depends on individual abilities but also on individuals' status and scope of action. Not only can high-status people express anger more freely than low status people (Burkitt, 2014; Rosenwein, 2020), it is also easier for high-status people to refrain from expressing anger – because they could if they wanted to and because they have other outlets further down the road. Secondly, the ability to align anger with the situation at hand and combine it with a problem-solving interest makes the disruptive function of anger more complex, since it does not necessarily promote superficial analyses and decision-making. Following anger within the context of these formal rituals, we can see that high-status professionals are able to channel the energy boost provided by anger to further their problem-solving abilities, while keeping the shallow information processing associated with anger in check. Here we can see some similarities with Nussbaum's depiction of Transition-Anger, which alerts one to an injustice, produces energy to find solutions, and involves a transition out of anger to "focusing on creating future welfare" (2016: 29). However, in contrast to Nussbaum's route from anger to non-anger, the legal professionals in our study transition in and out of anger as appropriate in the situation. It seems that when high status allows for anger to be expressed and formal rituals offer the means to channel it through established procedures, anger can play a distinct and systematic role in the legal process.

In reference to the formal rituals at play in the legal process, it is important to note that the ability of legal professionals to control their anger is facilitated by the fact that, in specific court situations, the court ritual allows them to press the pause button. Judges in particular, but also other legal actors, can interrupt, delay, or postpone the court process and thus generate space and time to adjust their anger in appropriate ways. This ability to move in and out of the interaction differentiates professional anger in court from anger in many other interactions that demand an immediate response, but it may be similar to professional anger paths in other bureaucratic organisations.

The criminal justice process is based on a rationalised temporal order or a "temporal anchoring of normalcy" (Zerubavel, 1985: 20). In court, the 'normal' is strictly regulated, while the matters that take people to court are out of the ordinary. On the one hand, the strict regularity of the legal process has been formed explicitly to deal with the irregularity of the matters examined in court in a structured way, bringing order to them. On the other hand, the irregularities of these matters, and the emotional intensity that they sometimes stir up, lead them to violate the expectation of 'normalcy' and thereby pave the way for anger. While we found the same basic logic of anger in all the countries examined with regard to what legal professionals get angry about and how anger aligns temporally with situations and problem-solving, we also found that anger takes on different meanings and values (Rosenwein, 2020: 21) depending on the emotional regime and legal tradition in which the feeling comes into play.

Institutional anger

Since our overarching aim with this book has been to explore rational anger, interpreted as the way anger is employed systematically in the court process, it is no surprise that we have found anger to be motivated by procedural rules and regulations, structuring and steering irritation in different ways depending on the rules that apply in the respective countries. In other words, we found legal anger to be structured by the professional culture of the different judicial systems.

The United States and Scotland have elaborate rules for how evidence should be presented, making legal professionals prone to anger when witnesses, in the context of examinations, do not limit their talk to what they have seen and heard but also include their interpretations. In Italy and Sweden, that follow the freedom of evidence principle, professionals do not become provoked by such accounts, and anger is instead generated by other forms of procedural rule-breaking. In Italy, professionals frequently get angry when witnesses fail to first look at the person who is posing the question and then turn to the judge to answer, and in Sweden, witnesses are reprimanded if they look at the opposing party when giving their testimony. Although these detailed and differing rules governing how stories are told in court vary across countries, they all share the fact that they diverge from the way stories are told in everyday life. Lay people in all countries often fail to follow legal storytelling requirements, which generates legal professional anger.

We also found that the same legal principle may give rise to different behavioural rules, which influences the implications of anger in more complex ways. For example, while the principle of impartiality implies that Swedish judges should not say anything that could negatively influence the defendant's case during a trial, this is not considered problematic for judges in the United States. US judges can express their anger about inappropriate charges or deficient arguments openly in court without risking their impartiality, whereas Swedish judges' anger about the same issues makes them vulnerable to criticism, producing anger tinged with anxiety. By comparing legal anger, we can trace differences in the logic and practice of impartiality in different legal systems.

Moral anger of different kinds

Anger always arises from a sense that something is unjustly wrong, but this wrong does not necessarily carry moral connotations. When we looked more closely into the explicitly moral underpinnings of legal professional anger, we found that the primary source of moral anger among legal professionals is linked to ensuring a correct legal process (legal pathos), and that expressions of moral outrage (condemnation of offences) were few and often subtle. Legal pathos trumped moral outrage in all four countries. Nevertheless, moral outrage was more openly displayed in the United States and Scotland than in Sweden and Italy. In the countries with a common law tradition (the United States and Scotland), moral outrage is to some extent institutionalised through its inclusion in sentencing decisions and the way these decisions are delivered. Judges openly present moral evaluations as part of their motivations for sentencing, and also direct moral speeches at defendants when presenting decisions about guilt. Judges working in civil law systems (Italy and Sweden) also make moral speeches, primarily in trials involving youths but only once the verdict and sentence have been delivered. In civil law systems, the emphasis on the application of law makes any goal-related aim suspicious. Judges and prosecutors should correctly follow process without any desire to lean towards a specific outcome, and the way Swedish and Italian judges distance themselves from moral evaluations in their work illustrates the importance they place on keeping their eyes on the process rather than the outcome. Legal encoding determines whether a case can proceed to court or a defendant should be found guilty, in effect decoupling moral judgement from legal judgment, and guilt in a moral sense from guilt in the legal sense.

In sum, the common law emphasis on interpreting and developing law, linking legal practice to current moral standards, also makes moral evaluations and outrage prevalent in legal practice in ways that are deemed unacceptable in civil law systems. However, in our material, moral anger is a complex affair, since it can take different routes towards retaliation, recognition, or resignation.

Retaliation, recognition, or resignation

Although previous theorising has integrated retaliation into the very definition of anger (Deonna and Teroni, 2015; Nussbaum, 2016), we only saw open retaliatory displays in our data from the United States, such as motivating a legal move to seek a harsh penalty by moral outrage at the criminal act of a defendant. According to Rosenwein (2020: 50–51), the idea that morally suspect behaviour should be avenged turns crimes into "insults", and a "sense that our honor has been insulted and maligned" (176).

This idea of insulted honour also emerged in the few examples of retaliatory aims that we found in the other countries, although here retaliation was not linked to the crime but to lay or professional behaviour during the trial. When retaliation is aimed at other legal professionals, it often takes the form of a subtle status degradation (Garfinkel, 1956; Nussbaum, 2016), such as when judges fantasise about putting the prosecutor down in their written verdicts. Here, retaliatory actions or imaginations occur when people in relatively higher status positions are hindered or offended by people in lower status positions whom they are nevertheless dependent on. According to Nussbaum (2016: 29), the idea of restoring status by diminishing the status of the other rests on a "narcissistic error", since it reduces wrongs or being hurt to a problem of relative position. From a rational perspective, too much focus on the self and on one's status undermines the legal professional tasks of solving legal problems and taking decisions (cf. Barbalet, 1998: 49). When judges write a mean sentencing opinion, it might give them a sense of satisfaction but it does not help them overcome the problem that made them angry in the first place.

The examples we find in Sweden and Italy involve legal professionals wanting to retaliate against what they consider to be obstructions to the legal procedure rather than against morally offensive crimes. When judges in Italy were reluctant to give a defendant a standard mitigatory sentence reduction, it was because the defendant had told the court a lot of 'nonsense' during trial, not because his offence was morally outrageous. In this last example, payback is not about status but is rather an expression of the perception that someone lacks respect for the legal professional or the court. Summing up, all forms of retaliation are rare in our material, particularly with regard to moral outrage at criminal acts, whereas retaliatory aims to restore the status (quo) are somewhat more common but often very subtle or only as a fantasy.

A more common avenue for anger found in our material involves an aim to achieve recognition (Lorde, 1997; Silva, 2024), which is often interpreted as merely stopping the action that gave rise to anger in the first place. When prosecutors or judges become angry at defendants or witnesses who do not give testimony in the way expected by the court, their anger fades as soon as these people follow their instructions. In contrast to the lingering anger that can result in retaliatory aims, here the problem gets solved and the legal professionals no longer need to be angry.

But aiming for recognition can also pave the way for determination. When judges become morally outraged by the vulnerability of defendants or victims, they generally do not express retaliatory inclinations but make efforts to provide care for the fragile parties through their choice of sentence. In the same vein, legal anger can energise judges and prosecutors into getting unruly lay people to come to court, trying to restore justice rather than get payback. These last examples are interesting, since in these situations, anger displayed a joyfulness that often is linked to retaliation in terms of the sweetness of revenge. However, here joy seemed rather to be linked to a feeling of righteousness, having used anger to restore something that had gone wrong (cf. Lorde, 1997), which demonstrates that anger-related joy need not necessarily be linked to retribution.

A third route of moral anger, which we only saw in Sweden, was resignation. While retaliation and recognition generate emotional energy to manage upcoming problems or situations, resignation produces a drop in energy, resulting in a lack of drive. Judges' moral outrage at having to make decisions that they think fail to deliver justice can engender a moral obligation to give up in order to distance themselves from their moral outrage. In the same vein, legal professionals' moral anger at other professionals who do not do a good job of defending the rule of law can give rise to disappointment and resignation (cf. Thagard, 2008: 168). Both these examples demonstrate high demands to discard moral evaluations altogether and to align one's feelings with legal pathos and dispassion.

The different paths that anger can take also raises the question of how anger can transition from or into other emotions. While Nussbaum's (2016) normative depiction of anger stresses transitions out of outrage into efforts to make things better without feeling angry, we find that anger can come from and lead into a diverse set of emotions in the legal setting.

Anger entangled

Our understanding of anger in this book has been inclusive. We have found examples of dislike and disapproval of various kinds, such as frustration, irritation, indignation, resentment, contempt, and outrage. These different flavours of anger provide important clues into its interpretative frames. While irritation and frustration both connote the blocking of goals, the latter signals recurrent problems. Both resentment and contempt indicate long-term hostility towards a person or a group rather than an individual problem or situation. Indignation represents anger on someone else's behalf, while outrage links to moral evaluations. These words in themselves can change in meaning both over time (Rosenwein, 2020) and in translation (Dixon, 2020), but in our study, they convey differences in meaning-making and approaches to the angering problem. In other words, anger is a complex bundle including transitions within the feeling itself. But anger also transitions from and into other emotions.

A common route into anger for legal professionals is via *surprise*, a response to unexpected events or information (Scott, 2021). The meeting between a strictly regulated legal procedure and the dramatic and often messy events that take people to court paves the way for surprise in the everyday work of legal professionals, and it has even been described as an expected and ordinary emotion (Bergman Blix and Wettergren, 2018). Surprising disruptions do not mix well with high expectations of regularity and rule-following and therefore tend to induce anger. But the focus in court is directed at stalling the situation, avoiding the risk of turning surprise into professional shame by reacting too quickly and thus failing to follow the correct rules. For this reason, legal professionals often appear passive in the face of surprises in court, relegating their anger to backstage arenas.

Another common emotion that instead works to counter anger is *patience* (Roach Anleu and Mack, 2021). Patience is used to control, or at least tone down, anger and irritation when lay people speak too much about legally irrelevant matters or too little about legally relevant matters. Patience is not only an empathic tool that allows lay people to tell their stories in court but also a legal tool for gaining enough information to evaluate relevance and credibility. Many cases rely on lay people's narratives, and the emotional investment of legal professionals in this reliance puts the balancing act between when to listen patiently and when to cut stories short, or when to manage and when to express anger, in the front seat.

A more contested emotion in court is *sympathy*, caring for someone else's suffering (Törnqvist, 2022). While sympathy can be used strategically by opposing parties in court to influence the likelihood of a favourable outcome for a client (Kusenbach and Loseke, 2013), it is viewed as jeopardising impartiality and puts legal professionals on their guard via feelings of annoyance and irritation. In these situations, irritation creates a distance to sympathetic feelings and gives rise to an ability to revise and scrutinise narratives or evidence that are perceived as being twisted by emotional manipulation. The combination of sympathy and annoyance can further breed distrust and suspicion towards those who tried to arouse one's sympathy in the first place, making "sympathy contests" (Kusenbach and Loseke, 2013) a daring game in court proceedings.

As has already been hinted at, anger resulting from surprise and sympathy, and also the patience to counter anger, all hinge on underlying threats of professional *shame*. The clear and strict court ritual, with limited room for deviations, makes episodes of full-blown shame rare, but shame instead appears in the background in the form of "trigger-warnings" (Bergman Blix and Wettergren, 2018: 22) to avoid potentially unprofessional behaviour and the risk of being accused of insincerity and incompetence (Hawley, 2017). When threats of shame are institutionalised into the legal ritual, for example, in the form of twisted narratives, they are often met with outright anger and dismissal, as when judges or prosecutors strongly reject attempts to manipulate stories. When the ability to manoeuvre around others' perceived wrongdoing is circumscribed by legal rules or traditions, the shame trigger comes closer and anger can instead signal diminished confidence and nervousness about how to move forward.

In the longer term, prevailing anger can influence feelings of confidence in the task and generate distrust towards individuals or the occupational group that gave rise to these feelings in the first place. On the other hand, in retrospective reflections, moments of insecurity and worry during the unfolding of a situation are often eliminated in favour of interpreting feelings of irritation and anger as being linked to certainty and determination. Once the messy and uncertain situation has been settled and the decision has been made, the emotions are put in order. Nussbaum (2016: 54) suggests that "narcissistic vulnerability", that is an exaggerated focus on the ego, can be reduced by following Aristotle's advice to contain anger with a "light-hearted and playful temper". This advice is apparently difficult to follow in the heat of the moment but seems nevertheless to be used as a means of reproducing professional confidence in retrospect.

Finally, one can ask why it is important to follow the paths of anger in and out of neighbouring emotions. Emotions seldom come in neatly separated bundles in real life situations, and following their routes provides a more accurate picture of their workings. This is important since it opens up for an understanding of the possible patterning of emotional processes. Does the institutional, in this case legal or perhaps bureaucratic, context pattern the evolving emotional processes by encouraging certain emotional routes and discouraging others? As we have shown, in legal, bureaucratic institutions, surprise opens up for anger as a result of the high demands placed on following correct procedure. One could speculate that in artistic institutions and creative occupations, surprise might instead induce feelings of flow rather than anger, since an openness to new angles and perspectives lies at the heart of creativity. In academia, these two avenues are potentially more balanced; surprise may open up for anger when robust methodologies are at risk, while being seen as more positive in relation to the generation of novel theoretical perspectives. Similarly, for prosecutors, surprise can be a welcome emotion during preliminary investigations, when new angles and perspectives can be productive to further the investigation, while, as corroborated here, surprise often instigates anger during court hearings (Törnqvist and Wettergren, 2023).

What is rational in legal anger?

The findings in this study highlight that legal anger can be perceived as 'rational' in many different ways. According to a commonsensical understanding of rationality, anger in court is rational when it is used deliberatively to pursue a legitimate legal goal. However, many of our examples of legal anger are not the product of reasoned or deliberate thought, but rather constitute emotional reactions to problems that arise. Conventionally, action is seen as non-rational when it is motivated by intuitive, emotional, or volitional grounds. But as our empirical examples demonstrate, even if an action is not embedded in rational reason, it can still fulfil rational aims and goals. According to this take on rationality, the question of whether or not acting on anger is rational will depend on the situation rather than the emotion. Using this framework, whether or not legal anger is rational depends on how it relates to overarching legal intentions and ambitions.

A related aspect of rational anger that we have used as a vantage point in this book involves the way anger is made rational in the everyday solving of legal problems in our courts. While most of the legal professionals in our material reject anger as a viable legal emotion, their legal practices demonstrate that anger is often coherent with the legal system per se. The patterns found in the reasons used to motivate legal anger speak to a systematic structure and the potential utility of legal anger. The way legal anger is used by the judges and prosecutors in this study rhymes well with the idea of rationality being used as a tool for selecting between different solutions, an intuitive weighting of alternatives. This is to say that from the legal professionals' point of view, anger makes sense and can be perceived as rational. This 'inside' outlook on anger as a professional means opens up for a view that the rationality of anger is dependent not only on situation but also on perspective.

So far we have avoided taking a normative stance, but to push the question of what is rational in anger further we need to integrate several perspectives to problematise its use and consequences. If we instead proceed from the point of view of defendants, plaintiffs, and witnesses, the rationality of legal anger discussed earlier is thrown off balance. Regardless how rational legal anger may seem from the legal professionals' perspective, being the target of outbursts of anger can be frightening, insulting, or simply incomprehensible. As an emotion that signals "a move against" (Miceli and Castelfranchi, 2019: 16), legal anger contradicts, or at least shakes, a core foundation of legal processes, namely that of treating people with respect. Several studies have emphasised the importance of legal professionals affording lay people the support they need to achieve a fair trial, regardless of whether the focus is on defendants (Hunter, 2005; Moorhead, 2007) or plaintiffs (Rock, 1991; Konradi, 1997; Schuster and Propen, 2010).

This shift in perspective leads us to the notion of procedural justice. Since legal institutions build on trust and legitimacy, procedural justice advances this idea by advocating that legal professionals should show respect, dignity, neutrality, and trustworthiness in legal encounters, and for the importance of being listened to as a lay person (Tyler and Bies, 1990; Tyler and Huo, 2002). If legal encounters meet these ends and are perceived as fair, they are more likely to result in compliance and deference on the part of the involved parties. The research on procedural justice shows that lay people's trust in the motives of legal professionals is not only key to the interactional dynamic in these encounters but also "shapes people's broader, long-term relationship to law and legal institutions" (Tyler and Huo, 2002: xv). When legal professionals use their anger and authority to put defendants, plaintiffs, or witnesses 'in their place', it can backfire and result in reduced trust in legal institutions and reduced compliance with actual judgements. Although its aim is to secure civil and smooth court proceedings or to distil the legal prerequisites from a messy lay narrative, anger can be perceived as unfair or unwarranted.

In other words, perspective matters and needs to be thoroughly scrutinised and reflected upon. As this book shows, in many instances, legal anger stems from legal pathos and a plea for recognition. In indignation and other forms of solidarity anger, these two elements extend the realm of legal anger and go beyond the legal professionals' individualistic rationales of restoring status or gaining the information required to reach fair and well-considered decisions. When legal anger encompasses an emancipatory concern, a passion that can be felt by the lay persons involved in court, it may promote procedural justice rather than restraining it. In court, judges and prosecutors express indignation in situations where they perceive that lay persons are treated wrongly or unfairly, with these perceptions often being linked to face-threatening acts (Goffman, 1967). According to Miceli and Castelfranchi (2019: 19), indignation constitutes "a moral response to the wrongs suffered by other people" and is thus a feeling that connects us to the situation of others. In this regard, there are clear overlaps between indignation and sympathy. Feeling indignation and acting on it is intended to reaffirm and restore the normative order. The urge to publicly condemn and penalise wrongdoing adds a collectivistic dimension to indignation as it aims to restore the norm itself, that is, social order and fairness (see also Cova et al., 2013) making legal professionals attentive to the boundaries of lay persons' (defendants', plaintiffs', and witnesses') integrity in court. At this applied level, the ability to change perspective and to link emotions into processes as discussed within the procedural justice framework can give rise to professional reflection about alternatives or best practices. On the other hand, professional anger in our material overwhelmingly aims to promote just and sound decisions, stressing the importance of balancing fair procedure with a fair outcome. In the end, the question of the rationality of anger is not as neat and tidy in real life. Our legal aims come in plural, manifold and changing over time, sometimes aligning with other goals and values, sometimes creating tension and ambivalence regarding what path to take.

The bigger picture

Lastly, we need to take a step back to place legal anger within the larger cultural and societal contexts in which it occurs. How can we understand the different routes of anger towards retaliation, recognition, or resignation and the different ways that anger is expressed in our four countries? Since 1981, the World Values Survey (WVS; www.worldvaluessurvey.org) has investigated beliefs and values across the globe, finding that two broad dimensions – traditional versus secular-rational values and survival versus self-expression values – largely explain the cultural variations between different countries around the world. In short, the traditional versus secular-rational dimension captures attitudes towards religion, deference to authority, and belief in traditional family values, while the survival versus self-expression dimension captures the degree of tolerance, trust, economic and physical security, and individual autonomy. The Inglehart-Welzel Cultural Map (WVS, 2023) illustrates the findings of the WVS, and on the basis of this map, Italy, Sweden, the United States, and Great Britain are relatively close to one another in a global perspective, but the countries are also characterised by distinctly different societal and cultural premises. While the countries in our study are located in three different culture zones identified in the WVS: Italy in Catholic Europe, Sweden in Protestant Europe, and the United States and Scotland in the English-speaking cluster, the Inglehart-Welzel map demonstrates that Sweden and Scotland (or Great Britain) are closer to one another in terms of their values than they are to Italy and the United States. In parallel, Italy and the United States share more similarities than the other countries in our study.

Sweden is an interesting case since it can be perceived as an international outlier and scores particularly high on both secular-rational and self-expression values compared to our other three countries (and the rest of the world). In addition, Sweden stands out with regard to a specific subset of self-expression values, so-called emancipative values. Emancipative values emphasise human autonomy and choice, the promotion of equality, and well-developed individual rights. These cultural values are strongly linked to socio-economic development, with rich countries scoring higher on secular-rational and self-expression values than poorer countries (Inglehart, 2018). With its strong roots in a social democratic welfare system and a tradition of redistributive policies, Sweden scores high on trust between people and social institutions (Haerpfer et al., 2022). Taken together, the combination of these cultural values and redistributive policies promotes ideals of inclusion rather than retaliation. When someone has wandered outside the moral boundaries of society, they should be re-integrated. Along with strong norms of consensus (Daun, 1996) that exert a pull towards compromise rather than conflict, this could explain the subtleness of angry expressions of any kind in Swedish courts in particular (Bergman Blix and Wettergren, 2016; Flower, 2020), and also the lack or hiding of retaliatory thoughts and actions. The civil law system's emphasis on correct procedure in a secular society strengthens the aversion against moral outrage – the law should evaluate evidence, not morality.

Moral anger, it seems, loses in rationality since it serves no clear function in the legal process. When Swedish legal professionals engage in moral outrage, they are more likely to move towards resignation than retaliation as a means of defusing unwa(rra)nted moral anger. However, societies are never static and an increased focus on punitive measures in the Swedish political sphere over the last decades (Pratt, 2008; Estrada et al., 2012) seems also to have opened the door to a retaliatory discourse in court, at least in the prosecutorial vocabulary, where depictions of "evil" defendants might signal a change towards retributive aims.[1] For judges, the combination of a procedural focus on correct procedure and the adversarial call for a passive judge might make the step towards open moral expression greater.

In comparison, the United States is marked by a strong foundation of traditional values unsurpassed by any other post-industrial country (except Ireland), particularly underscoring the importance of religion and national pride (Inglehart and Welzel, 2005), but it also scores high on self-expression. The combination of traditional values regarding religion, family, and deference to authority and self-expressive values of tolerance, security, and individual autonomy makes the United States an outlier in relation to other rich countries, which tend to be moving away from traditional values. If Sweden is an outlier due to its high levels on both scales, the United States is an outlier due to its unusual combination of values. This can be seen in the strong ideals of individual freedom (the American dream) along with the traditional values found in US politics that emphasise trust in family and the church rather than in the state (Haerpfer et al., 2022). The moral boundaries associated with traditional religious values, along with socio-economic conditions that emphasise that individuals must stand on their own feet, possibly opens up for retaliatory anger as a response to feeling wronged. Nussbaum's retaliatory anger is clearly situated in the US value system, where "the rich w[ould] be upset and pained" if they were to pay more taxes to alleviate the situation of "the poor" (2016: 37). For the courts, the political election of prosecutors general as well as judges (in some states) serves to pull political goals such as being 'tough on crime' closer to legal practice than in countries where the political and the judicial branches are more clearly separated. Common law judges in both the United States and Scotland express individual power (Remiche, 2015) more clearly, as is depicted in their standard references to 'my court', which possibly opens up for expressions of anger. An interesting contrast to the other countries is that the rebukes from judges in US courts at

1 Historically, certain crimes have gained a lot of media attention and elicited moral outrage in the public sphere. While prosecutors and other legal professionals usually maintain a neutral stance in the media coverage, they sometimes express moral outrage. One case that could be considered a game-changer was the so-called "Malexander murders", when two police officers were murdered in 1999 following a bank robbery. In a recent case of gross child abuse (Lund District Court, case B 6683/22), the prosecutor, in her closing argument, called for long sentences due to the abuse having been "pure evil" (Hansson, 2024).

times stand out in their use of informal language ("Y'ALL", "*who cares!*", etc.), perhaps signalling class as a changing rather than stable condition.[2]

Since our limited data from Scotland do not make it possible to find patterns in legal anger in the same way as in the other three countries, we will only make a few short remarks related to Scotland's cultural and societal context. Scotland (or Great Britain, since the WVS map does not include potential within country differences) scores comparably close to Sweden in both rational-secular and self-expressive values but lies a little further away in relation to self-expressive values, potentially indicating lower levels of ideals of equality promotion and redistribution (emancipatory values). Class remains very present in British society at large and even more so in the judiciary (Reeves and Friedman, 2024) and the limited data we have from Scotland contain manifestations of strong class markers, where expression of contempt may constitute one such example.

Italy is located a little higher on secular values but lower on self-expression values compared to the United States. In the overall picture, both Italy and the United States score lower on both these dimensions than Sweden and Scotland (WVS., 2023). The high levels of traditional values may be reflected in the many examples we have of angry expressions directed at uncooperative victims of intimate partner violence (IPV) in Italy, where the criminalisation of IPV came comparatively late (Sette, 2023). But at first sight, our data from Italy seem to challenge the link between secular values, socio-economic welfare, and (lack of) retaliatory aims in court (as argued in the Swedish case). According to this logic, Italy's strong traditional values, compared to Sweden and Great Britain, along with a less developed welfare system, should encourage retributive aims. This might be true in everyday life, but, in addition to the overall moral distancing incorporated into the civil law tradition, the fact that legal institutions in Italy are more clearly decoupled from political institutions than in the United States seems to play a greater role in keeping retaliatory aims out of the courts. The decoupling of legal and political institutions in Italy has historical roots in the period during which most of the participants in our material embarked on their legal careers, namely the period of the 'Mani pulite' investigations in Italy during the early '90s, which led to a 'revolution of the judges' (Della Porta et al., 2013).[3] As described by our Italian participants, the strong anti-corruption sentiments of this time generated a powerful sense of pride and legal pathos in ensuring the correctness of the legal process and in representing the state against (corrupted) politics.[4] In contrast to Sweden, where resignation is a (desired) route

2 In data from all selected countries, the majority of judges self-reported as middle or upper-middle class but with more examples of working-class background from the United States.

3 Mani pulite (clean hands) was a nationwide investigation into political corruption in Italy in the 1990s.

4 More recent research suggests that the courts were given too big a role in tackling corruption, and when politicians, first led by Berlusconi, fought back and dismissed anti-corruption judgements as politically motivated, corruption soon took off again (Vannucci, 2009).

for moral anger, the urge to balance legal pathos and moral outrage against corruption is to some extent stronger in Italy, where indignation is expected to a greater extent.

Although our arguments remain sketchy, we can see that the different expressions and routes of anger in the countries and legal systems examined, towards retaliation, recognition, or resignation make sense within the cultural and socio-economic systems in which they appear. It is also clear that whether the legal tradition pertains to civil law or common law matters the most for how morality enters the process in the first place.

Concluding remarks

We started this book by stating that while anger is a demanding companion, it may sometimes be necessary to the pursuit of rational goals. Although anger is often perceived as interruptive and uncompromising, we have found that anger can be conducive to, and systematically patterned in, the legal process. In other words, legal anger can promote sensibly energetic rather than disruptive actions and can involve remaining calm and setting out to meet rational ends. Early theorising on rational emotions emphasised rationality as feeling focused, decisive, and at ease (James, 1879), much in line with Aristotle's call for 'light-heartedness'. Although anger hardly qualifies as 'light-hearted', its decisive energy and deliberateness carry rational qualities. Legal anger is intrinsically linked to the experience of having one's agency diminished and to central legal values being damaged. When legal professionals are passionate about their work (as opposed to indifferent), they are also bound to become angry about failures of justice.

References

Barbalet Jack. (1998) *Emotion, Social Theory, and Social Structure—A Macrosociological Approach*. Cambridge: Cambridge University Press.

Bergman Blix Stina and Minissale Alessandra. (2022) (Dis)passionate law stories: The emotional processes of encoding narratives in court. *Journal of Law and Society* 49: 245–262.

Bergman Blix Stina and Wettergren Åsa. (2016) A sociological perspective on emotions in the judiciary. *Emotion Review* 8: 32–37.

Bergman Blix Stina and Wettergren Åsa. (2018) *Professional Emotions in Court: A Sociological Perspective*. London: Routledge.

Burkitt Ian. (2014) *Emotions and Social Relations*. London: SAGE.

Cova Florian, Deonna Julien and Sander David. (2013) The emotional shape of our moral life: Anger-related emotions and mutualistic anthropology. *Behavioral and Brain Sciences* 36: 86–87.

Daun Åke. (1996) *The Swedish Mentality*. University Park: The Pennsylvania State University Press.

Deflem Mathieu. (2008) *Sociology of Law – Visions of a Scholarly Tradition*. Cambridge: Cambridge University Press.

Della Porta Donatella, Vannucci Alberto and Wilson Alex. (2013) Corruption and anti-corruption: The political defeat of 'clean hands' in Italy. In: MJ Bull and M Rhodes (eds) *Italy – A Contested Polity*. London: Routledge, 174–197.

Deonna Julien A and Teroni Fabrice. (2015) Emotions as attitudes. *dialectica* 69: 293–311.

Dixon Thomas. (2020) What is the history of anger a history of? *Emotions: History, Culture, Society* 4: 1–34.

Estrada Felipe, Pettersson Tove and Shannon David. (2012) Crime and criminology in Sweden. *European Journal of Criminology* 9: 668–688.

Flower Lisa. (2020) *Interactional Justice: The Role of Emotions in the Performance of Loyalty*. Abingdon, Oxon: Routledge.

Garfinkel Harold. (1956) Conditions of successful degradation ceremonies. *The American Journal of Sociology* 61: 420–424.

Goffman Erving. (1959) *The Presentation of Self in Everyday Life*. New York: Doubleday.

Goffman Erving. (1967) *Interaction Ritual. Essays on Face-to-Face Behavior*. New York: Pantheon Books.

Hansson Tove. (2024) Åklagaren vill se långa fängelsestraff för föräldrarna till ättiksförgiftade flickan: "Ren ondska" (The prosecutor requests long sentences for the parents of the acid-poisoned girl: "Pure evil"). *Dagens Nyheter*.

Haraway Donna. (1988) Situated knowledges: The science question in feminism and the privilege of partial perspective. *Feminist studies* 14: 575–599.

Harding Sandra. (1992) Rethinking standpoint epistemology: What is "strong objectivity"? *The Centennial Review* 36: 437–470.

Haerpfer Christian, Inglehart Ronald F, Moreno Alejandro, et al. (2022) Confidence in Government, In: M Lagos, P Norris, E Ponarin, et al. (eds) *World Values Survey: Round seven – Country-Pooled Datafile Version 5.0*. Madrid, Spain: JD Systems Institute & WVSA Secretariat.

Hawley Katherine. (2017) Trust, distrust, and epistemic injustice. In: IJ Kidd, J Medina and G Pohlhaus (eds) *The Routledge Handbook of Epistemic Injustice*. Abingdon: Routledge, 69–78.

Hunter Rosemary. (2005) Styles of judging: How magistrates deal with applications for intervention orders. *Alternative Law Journal* 30: 231–246.

Inglehart Ronald F. (2018) *Cultural Evolution*. Cambridge: Cambridge University Press.

Inglehart Ronald and Welzel Christian. (2005) *Modernization, Cultural Change, and Democracy: The Human Development Sequence*. Cambridge: Cambridge University Press.

James William. (1879) The sentiment of rationality. *Mind* 4: 317–346.

Jones Bryan D. (1999) Bounded rationality. *Annual Review of Political Science* 2: 297–321.

Kalberg Stephen. (1980) Max Weber's types of rationality: Cornerstones for the analysis of rationalization processes in history. *American Journal of Sociology* 85: 1145–1179.

Konradi Amanda. (1997) Too little, too late: Prosecutors' pre-court preparation of rape survivors. *Law & Social Inquiry* 22: 1–54.

Kusenbach Margarethe and Loseke Donileen R. (2013) Bringing the social back in: Some suggestions for the qualitative study of emotions. *Qualitative Sociology Review* 9: 20–38.

Lorde Audre. (1997) The uses of anger. *Women's Studies Quarterly* 25: 278–285.

Miceli Maria and Castelfranchi Cristiano. (2019) Anger and its cousins. *Emotion Review* 11: 13–26.

Moorhead Richard. (2007) The passive arbiter: Litigants in person and the challenge to neutrality. *Social & Legal Studies* 16: 405–424.
Nordquist Cecilia Y and Bergman Blix Stina. (2022) Expanding emotional capital in court. *Frontiers in Sociology* 7: 1–12.
Nussbaum Martha C. (2016) *Anger and Forgiveness: Resentment, Generosity, Justice.* Oxford: Oxford University Press.
Pratt John. (2008) Scandinavian exceptionalism in an era of penal excess. *British Journal of Criminology* 48: 275–292.
Reeves Aaron and Friedman Sam. (2024) *Born to Rule: The Making and Remaking of the British Elite.* London: Harvard University Press.
Remiche Adélaïde. (2015) When judging is power: A gendered perspective on the French and American judiciaries. *Journal of Law and Courts* 3: 95–113.
Roach Anleu Sharyn and Mack Kathy. (2021) *Judging and Emotion: A Socio-Legal Analysis.* Abingdon, Oxon: Routledge.
Rock Paul. (1991) Witnesses and space in a Crown Court. *British Journal of Criminology* 31: 266–279.
Rosenwein Barbara H. (2020) *Anger: The Conflicted History of an Emotion.* Yale: Yale University Press.
Scarduzio Jennifer A. (2011) Maintaining order through deviance? The emotional deviance, power, and professional work of municipal court judges. *Management Communication Quarterly* 25: 283–310.
Schuster Mary Lay and Propen Amy. (2010) Degrees of emotion: Judicial responses to victim impact statements. *Law, Culture and the Humanities* 6: 75–104.
Scott Susie. (2021) Surprise: A micro-sociological analysis. *Emotions and Society* 3: 191–207.
Sette Raffaella. (2023) Evolving legal landscape in the field of domestic abuse in Italy. *URBAN CRIME* 4: 60–75.
Silva Laura. (2024) Is anger a hostile emotion? *Review of Philosophy and Psychology* 15: 383–402.
Simon Herbert A. (1990) Bounded rationality. In: J Eatwell, M Milgate and P Newman (eds) *Utility and Probability.* London: Palgrave Macmillan, 15–18.
Thagard Paul. (2008) How cognition meets emotion: Beliefs, desires and feelings as neural activity. In: G Brun, U Doguoglu and D Kuenzle (eds) *Epistemology and Emotions.* Aldershot: Ashgate, 167–184.
Törnqvist Nina. (2022) Drizzling sympathy: Ideal victims and flows of sympathy in Swedish courts. *International Review of Victimology* 28: 263–285.
Törnqvist Nina and Wettergren Åsa. (2023) Epistemic emotions in prosecutorial decision-making. *Journal of Law and Society* 50: 208–230.
Tyler Tom R and Bies Robert J. (1990) Beyond formal procedures: The interpersonal context of procedural justice. *Applied Social Psychology and Organizational Settings* 77: 98.
Tyler Tom R and Huo Yuen J. (2002) *Trust in the Law: Encouraging Public Cooperation with the Police and Courts.* New York: Russell Sage Foundation.
Vannucci Alberto. (2009) The controversial legacy of 'mani pulite': A critical analysis of Italian corruption and anti-corruption policies. *Bulletin of Italian Politics* 1: 233–264.
WVS. (2023) The Inglehart-Welzel World Cultural Map - World Values Survey 7, Source: http://www.worldvaluessurvey.org/
Zerubavel Eviatar. (1985) *Hidden Rhythms: Schedules and Calendars in Social Life.* Berkeley: University of California Press.

Index

Note: Page numbers followed by "n" refer to notes.